Design your Intention

AN EXPERIENCE OF EMBODYING SOURCE

by

Ruth Ford-Crenshaw

Inner Eye Books

An Imprint of
OUGHTEN HOUSE PUBLICATIONS
LIVERMORE, CALIFORNIA, USA

Design Your Intention: An Experience of Embodying Source
by
Ruth Ford-Crenshaw
Published 1997

01 00 99 98 97   0 9 8 7 6 5 4 3 2
Copyright © 1997 Ruth Ford-Crenshaw

PUBLISHED BY:
INNER EYE BOOKS
an imprint of
OUGHTEN HOUSE PUBLICATIONS
P.O. BOX 2008
LIVERMORE, CALIFORNIA, 94551-2008 USA
PHONE: (510) 447-2332
FAX: (510) 447-2376
E-MAIL: oughtenhouse.com
WEBSITE: www.oughtenhouse.com

Library of Congress Cataloging-in-Publication Data
Ford-Crenshaw, Ruth, 1951-
    Design your intention: an experience of embodying source / by
Ruth Ford-Crenshaw.
        p.   cm.
    Includes bibliographical references.
    ISBN 1-880666-63-4 (pbk.)
    1. Self-realization.   2. I AM Religious Activity.   I. Title.
BP605.I18F67   1997
299'.93--dc21
                                                                97-5107
                                                                CIP

ISBN 1-880666-63-4, Trade Paperback
Printed in United States of America

Contents

Exercises

About the Author

Ruth Ford-Crenshaw is a unique combination of business savvy and spiritual awareness. Her successful 20-year business career and lifetime as a spiritual seeker includes: Co-Founder of one of the largest Denver real estate companies in the 1970s and Vice-President for the Denver division of Merrill Corporation, financial publishers. Ruth was the business manager for Nizhoni School for Global Consciousness, founded by Chris Griscom of The Light Institute of Galisteo, and is also a Light Body graduate and core group member of the program developed by Orin and DaBen, channeled by Sanaya Roman and Duane Packer.

Ruth recently reaccepted a seat on the Council of Twelve for the Trinity Foundation, organized by Dr. Norma Milanovich. She has also worked extensively with Brian Grattan, author of *Mahatma I & II.*

Most recently, Ruth established a nonprofit, tax-exempt organization called Divine Creations Foundation that sponsors books, tapes, and workshops of a metaphysical nature. *Design Your Intention* is her first book.

About the Cover

On the cover is the symbol of the Flower of Life in the process of being designed. A completed symbol consists of nineteen interconnecting circles, and can be found at ancient sites all round the world.

One of the cornerstones of Sacred Geometry is that all languages, all laws of physics, and all biological lifeforms are based on and contained within the Flower of Life.

Through understanding how the geometry works, the rational mind is able to grasp the reality of Oneness.

Publisher's Note

This book contains material from other authors, reprinted with permission and unedited. The material appears in a distinctive typeface.

Preface

When the moon was full in the month of May, 1996, I went to Mt. Shasta for the Wesak Festival sponsored by Dr. Joshua David Stone. While celebrating Buddha's moment of enlightenment, I became energetically infused with the desire to write this book. In the past, all my seminars and audio tapes have been generated by my mental body but the book you hold in your hands is a collaborative effort of heart, mind, and consciousness. In it I have used, with permission, the fine writings of other people. Their work is an important aspect of this book, for we learn from one another, so my intent was to build a platform to present a variety of work from those who have given me so much inspiration along the way.

This book is about spiritual transformation. The mechanism that triggers this expansion of consciousness to the point of self-realization is *intention*. Because of my discipline and work, Ascended Master St. Germain of the Spiritual Hierarchy of this planet asked me to be one of the Keepers of the Flame. I'm sure that being a Keeper takes on a different meaning for each individual; the words collected here reflect what being a Keeper of the Flame means to me.

St. Germain has been responsible for the safekeeping of the Violet Flame that transforms and transmutes. The results of using it are startling. Some of the many stories about St. Germain have focused on alchemy, defining it as turning base metal into gold or removing flaws from precious stones. But, in fact, the highest form of alchemy is the organic transformation of an individual from a carbon-based being into a being of Light in what is referred to as the ascension process. An evolving and enlightened being is one of the results, and the Violet Flame is one tool that can be used toward that end. To invoke the energy of the Violet Flame is to be engulfed by it as it transforms and transmutes accumulated energy that is less than perfection.

The other tool for transmutation is your *intention*, and you can specifically design your intention by selecting certain life experiences over others. This book is a record of a personal journey through the myriad openings that life offers, with key decisions being made within a larger blueprint for transformation. As you read this book, try to hold the big picture in your mind and see how the forks in the road presented themselves and how the choices were made within the larger context.

I read the following by Nelson Mandela every few days to provoke thought and to inspire me not to wither under the mundane tasks of everyday life:

> Our worst fear
> Is not that we are inadequate;
> Our deepest fear is that we are
> Powerful beyond measure.
> It is our light,
> Not our darkness, that most frightens us.
> We ask ourselves,
> "Who am I to be brilliant,
> Gorgeous, talented, and fabulous?"
> Actually, who are you not to be?
> You are a child of God;
> Your playing small doesn't serve the world.
> There is nothing enlightened about
> Shrinking so that other people
> Won't feel insecure around you.
> We were born to make manifest
> The glory of God within us.
> It is not just in some of us, it is in everyone.
> And as we let our own light shine,
> We unconsciously give other people
> Permission to do the same.
> As we are liberated from our own fear,
> Our presence automatically liberates others.

My intention is to share my experience and knowledge. If, in the process of reading this book, you stretch and decide to look at yourself from an expanded perspective, then I will have completed my assignment.

Introduction

Because most people can relate to the transformation of a caterpillar into a butterfly, I found this parable by Kryon* to exemplify the confusion surrounding transformation.

THE FUZZY CATERPILLAR

The forest was bustling with life, and underneath the low foliage canopy of the ground cover the big fuzzy caterpillar was speaking to his group of caterpillar followers. Not much had changed in the caterpillar community. The big fuzzy caterpillar's job was to watch over the group so that all the old ways were kept and respected. After all, they were sacred.

"Word has it," said the big fuzzy caterpillar between bites of his ever present leaf meal, "that there is a spirit of the forest who is offering caterpillars everywhere some big new deal." Munch, munch. "I have decided to meet with this spirit and advise you on what we are supposed to do."

"Where will you find the spirit?" said one of the followers.

"It will come to me," said the big fuzzy one. "After all...can't go too far, you know. No food beyond the grove. Can't be without food." Munch, munch.

So when the big caterpillar was alone, he called out loud for the spirit of the forest and in not too long a time the great quiet spirit came to him. The forest spirit was beautiful, but much was hidden since the caterpillar wasn't known to leave his cozy leaf bed. "I can't see your face very well" said the big caterpillar.

"Come a bit higher," said the spirit of the forest in a kind voice. "I am here for you to see." But the caterpillar remained where he was. After all, it was his house and the spirit of the forest was there by invitation.

"No thanks," said the big fuzzy one. "Too much trouble right now. Tell me, what's all this I hear about some big miracle that's only available to caterpillars...not ants or centipedes...just caterpillars?"

---

*   *The Fuzzy Caterpillar*, Kryon Quarterly, 1996. Reprinted by permission.

"It's true," said the spirit of the forest. "You have earned a gift that is amazing. And if you decide you want it, I will tell you how."

"How did we earn it?" said the fuzzy one, busy with his third leaf since the conversation started. " I don't remember signing up for anything."

"You earned it through your wonderful lifetime efforts to keep the forest sacred," said the spirit.

"You bet!" said the caterpillar. "I do that every day, every day. I'm the leader of the group, you know. That's why you are talking to me instead of just any caterpillar." At this comment, the forest spirit smiled at the caterpillar, although the caterpillar couldn't see it since he had decided not to get off his leaf. "I've been keeping the forest sacred now for a long time," said the caterpillar. "What do I get?"

"It's an amazing gift," replied the forest spirit. "You are now able, through your own efforts, to change into a beautiful winged creature and fly! Your colors will be amazing and your mobility will startle all who see you. You can go anywhere you wish in the forest by flying above it. You will be able to find food everywhere, and meet new beautiful winged creatures as well. All this you may do immediately if you wish."

"Caterpillars that fly!" mused the fuzzy one. "That's unbelievable! If this is true, then show me some of these flying caterpillars. I want to see them."

"It's easy," replied the spirit. "Just travel to a high place and look around you. They are everywhere, flitting from branch to branch, having a wonderful abundant life in the sun."

"Sun?" exclaimed the caterpillar. "If you really are the forest spirit, you know that sun is hot for us caterpillars...bakes us, it does...isn't good for our hair, you know...have to stay in the dark...nothing worse than a caterpillar with bad hair."

"When you change into the winged creature, the sun enhances your beauty," said the spirit kindly and patiently. "The old methods of your existence will change dramatically and you will leave the old caterpillar ways on the floor of the forest while you soar into the new ways of the winged ones."

The caterpillar was silent for a moment. "You want me to leave my comfortable bed here and travel to a high place in the sun to see proof?"

"If you need proof, that's what you have to do," replied the patient spirit.

"No," said the caterpillar. "Can't do that...have to eat, you know. Can't go to strange high places in the sun to gawk when there's work here. Too dangerous! Anyway, if you were the forest spirit you would know that caterpillars eyes point down, not up. The great Earth spirit gave us good eyes that point down so we can find food...any caterpillar knows that. What you ask isn't very caterpillar-like," said the increasing suspicious fuzzy one. "Looking up isn't something we do much of." The caterpillar was silent for a moment. "So how do we accomplish this flying thing?"

The spirit of the forest then explained the process of metamorphosis. He explained how the caterpillar had to commit to the change, since he could not reverse it after it started. He explained how the caterpillar used his own biology while in the cocoon to change into a winged creature. He explained how the change would require a sacrifice, a time of quiet darkness while in the cocoon until all was ready for the graduation into a beautiful multicolored flying creature. The caterpillar listened quietly, not interrupting except for the munching noises.

"Let me get this straight," the caterpillar finally said irreverently. "You want us all to lie down and give intent for some biological thing that we have never heard of to take us over. Then we are to let this new biological thing encase us totally in the dark for months?"

"Yes," remarked the spirit of the forest, knowing only too well where the conversation was going next.

"And you, as the great forest spirit, won't do this for us? We have to do it ourselves? I thought we earned it!"

"You earned it," said the spirit quietly. "And you also earned the power to change yourselves in the new forest energy. Even as you sit on your leaf, your own body is equipped to do it all."

"What happened to the days when food fell from heaven, waters parted, and the walls of cities fell down, stuff like that? I'm not stupid, you know. I may be big and fuzzy, but I've been around awhile. The spirit of the Earth always does the big work, and all we are supposed to do is follow instructions. Anyway, if we all did what you asked, we would starve! Any caterpillar knows that you have to eat all the time"...munch, munch..."to stay alive. Your big new deal sounds pretty suspicious to me."

The caterpillar thought for a moment and said "dismissed!" to the forest spirit, as he turned around to find where the next bite was coming from. The forest spirit quietly departed as asked, as he heard the caterpillar mumbling to himself, "Caterpillars that fly!! My left feet!" Munch, munch.

The next day the caterpillar issued a proclamation and gathered his followers together for a conference. All was still as the crowd listened intently to find out what the big fuzzy one had to say about their future.

"The spirit of the forest is evil!" proclaimed the caterpillar to his followers. "He wants to trick us into a very dark place where we will surely die. He wants us to believe that our own bodies will somehow turn us into flying caterpillars...all we have to do is stop eating for a few months!" Great laughter ensued at this remark.

"Common sense and history will show you how the great Earth spirit has always worked," continued the caterpillar. "No good spirit will ever take you to a dark place! No good spirit will ask you to do something so Godlike by yourself! These are the tricks of the great evil forest spirit." The caterpillar swelled up in self-importance, ready for the next comment. "I have met with the evil one and have recognized him!" The other caterpillars went wild with accolade, and carried the big fuzzy one on their smaller fuzzy backs around in circles while they gave him praise for saving them from a certain death.

We leave this festival of caterpillars and gently move up through the forest. As the commotion below begins to fade from our ears we pass through the canopy of leaves that shields the bottom of the forest from sunlight. We gently move up through the darkness of the leaves into the area reserved for those that can fly. Even as the din of celebrating caterpillars is gradually lost to our ears we experience the grandness of the winged ones. Flitting from tree to tree in the bright sunlight are multitudes of gloriously colored, free-flying caterpillars called butterflies, each one decked in the splendor of rainbow colors, some even that were former friends of the big fuzzy dark one below...each one with a smile and plenty to eat...each one transformed by the great gift from the spirit of the forest.

The only thing that stops us is fear. Fear has many different faces, but it is what holds everything in place.

There is only one Way to the Source. It is through the taking of a path or several paths that the Way opens up. A path may be called a particular religion, a philosophy, or a code to live by. A path assists in expanding the consciousness by presenting scenarios to an individual to learn from and move beyond. Another way of explaining this is that an individual works towards and then integrates a point of realization. When this expansion of consciousness or point of realization takes place, the ideas around the scenario and the space holding those ideas are transformed. This transformation allows Light to penetrate that space. True embodiment of the Source occurs in stages as we integrate points of realization infused with Light. Meanwhile, the heart opens, showing the Way to the full embodiment of the Source. This process creates the organic transformation into a being of Light.

The divine plan includes each small self embodied in a physical vehicle working through all the points of realization to the large Self which resides at the Source level, the large Self being the full embodiment of the Source. In this process of learning to integrate each point of realization, we learn that within each point of realization lies the understanding at increasingly deeper levels that we are one with the Source. Learning about this oneness is the process of enlightenment. It is a multifaceted process, much like the caterpillar's transformation into a butterfly.

PART 1:

The Story of My Spiritual Evolution

The Turning Point: Moving Me Beyond Traditional Beliefs

I was raised Roman Catholic. In the mid-1960s, my mother discovered Eckankar, a teaching of soul travel based on the guidance of the Eck masters. Eckankar became a way of life for my parents and they came to be considered high initiates in that organization. In fact, my father has been on the board of directors for many years.

During the 1970s, I attended several Eckankar gatherings and found myself becoming more and more interested in metaphysics (which means "beyond the physical"). At that time I didn't know of any other sources so I stayed on the fringes of Eckankar, reading primarily books purchased at their gatherings.

By 1980, I no longer resonated with Eckankar. In fact every organized group of any persuasion had become a turnoff. It seemed to me that most people involved in them simply needed to be connected with something. That made me uncomfortable because I unconsciously knew it was reflecting back my own need for a connection and I perceived that as a weakness.

Then in 1981, I had a most profound experience, the core of which took place in a lucid dream.

I had just moved into a condo with a roommate who was a friend of a close friend. I didn't know the woman at all but had been warned that she was deeply religious in the traditional sense, even encouraging her employees to read the Bible at work. I didn't care, as long as she didn't force her belief structure on me. Her name was Judy and she was a pleasant woman with a strong sense of herself and of God. She was a bit older than I and much more worldly.

I soon learned that being around someone who is totally devoted to God, no matter what form that devotion takes, affects a person on an energetic level. Her effect on me was a nonstop stirring within. I began reading books on a much broader range of topics, including theosophy, Madam Blavatsky, and a variety of Eastern philosophies. I became thoroughly confused because everyone seemed to use the same words but defined them differently.

I began having conversations with a male friend who was well versed in metaphysical and spiritual teachings. It was very stimulating because I had never before discussed metaphysics with anyone but Eckists. The wide range of information he had at his fingertips inspired me to learn as much as I could. Then Judy observed that my friend had ulterior motives, of which I was unaware, for sharing his knowledge. Judy told me in her gentle way that I had better open my eyes and not depend so much on someone else for validation. She said, in fact, that I had all I needed within myself. She also recommended a book called *Hind's Feet on High Places* by Hannah Hurnard.

One Saturday when I knew I would be alone all day, I curled up on the couch and began reading the book. Once I started, I couldn't stop. I found myself sobbing and calling to God for help in achieving true knowledge and wisdom because I realized I was very much like the main character in the book, Much Afraid.

Riddled with fear of the unknown and of making a mistake, Much Afraid doubted her ability to experience God or whether or not she would know how to go about it. She felt insignificant and undeserving. I, too, had been feeling these things for some time. Upon finishing the book, I was completely drained. I could no longer think or feel; all I could do was collapse into bed.

That night I had a lucid dream. I was asleep, yet totally awake, but every cell in my body was alert to what was going on. I saw before me a Tibetan man from the shoulders up. He had piercing eyes that turned into small blue flames. Then his whole being became a large blue flame. In an instant, the large blue flame shrank into a blue spark and disappeared.

It all happened quickly but it seemed to hang in non-time. It was more vivid and real to me than my everyday life. I spoke of the dream to no one because I knew it meant something important and I was afraid that no one would understand, or by discounting it, they would take away its significance for me. So I told no one and savored the experience for myself. In the years that followed, I came to realize that my Tibetan had not been the ascended master associated with Eckankar as I had originally assumed but rather he had been my higher self taking on a form I could accept.

Immediately after the dream, I noticed that every morning I would go to the bathroom and empty myself out for as long as twenty to thirty minutes. It became an everyday ritual for over two weeks. I thought maybe I had a touch of the flu or something and gave it no more thought. At the same time I began to observe that others reacted to me differently. I would go into the butcher shop and the owner would say, "If all my customers glowed like you do, it would be such a joy to do business." The manager of the condo complex where I lived said, "My goodness, you seem to light up this whole room," when I picked up my mail. My life seemed to flow with ease and grace. I wasn't even aware of my new state of being, however.

About a month later, I was returning home from a friend's wedding when a man in the elevator commented how nice it would be to find someone like me. His words caught me off guard and I found myself dwelling on the fact that I didn't have someone special in my life. It dashed me out of my new and glorious state of being.

I understand now what had happened. I'd had such a strong reaction to reading *Hind's Feet on High Places* that I had released something within my body, something that had been holding me back. It could have been the thought of not being connected to God, that feeling of separateness. What it was is irrelevant; what matters is that we carry within our physical bodies, in the form of stuck or dense energy, thoughts and feelings that hold us back and keep us from evolving. The thread that surrounds this dense energy and holds it in place is fear.

As the stuck energy was being released, something else was happening. By calling on God for help, I had set up the dynamic that made it possible for the soul and the spirit to come into unity, a process often called a soul merge. For that to occur, mental and emotional bodies have to come into alignment to some degree with the physical body, resulting in an increase in vibrational frequency. In order for my physical body to be able to handle the higher vibration, it had to let go of much of the physical matter within it; hence, the lengthy visits to the bathroom.

I allowed what the man in the elevator had said to trigger a release of energy in my body that had to do with unworthiness, thus creating a cycle of thoughts and emotions about why I wasn't in a relationship. This happens when we tap into stuck energy and unless we understand it, we remain caught in that cycle for some time.

In this cycle, the physical body reacts to the stuck energy of thoughts and feelings in the mental and emotional bodies, respectively, often creating an unbalance. The mental and emotional bodies are higher frequency energy fields surrounding the physical body and constantly interact with it. These bodies hold all thoughts and all feelings—the good as well as those we perceive as bad. I call that state of being the Path of Ease, a state in which we allow ourselves to be totally and absolutely in the flow at all times but don't think too much about it.

For a month nothing in my day-to-day activities or interactions caused me to reflect on my inner state. I experienced what it was like to live as my higher self. Once it was over, I longed for it to return. Behind the facade of our daily lives, we are in divine union with God and this experience taught me that when we suppress any part of our wholeness, we suppress part of our divinity. Wholeness is all that I am in existence, not just here but in other dimensions or realities where there may be no time, space, or form as we know it. Yet an energy that is me exists there. All that I am within my wholeness is a divine expression of God. Because I am a part of God, my wholeness reflects that divinity, including all aspects of humanness. By not accepting the part of myself that felt unworthy, I was suppressing a part of my divinity.

A Time of Experimentation

A couple of uneventful years passed until I went on vacation to Mexico, where I happened to meet a psychic named Linda Schiller. I resonated with her because she took her gift beyond what I had always imagined as the psychic realms. My impression of psychics had always been that while they gave readings that told of events, past or present, they mainly gave guidance pertaining to future events. I felt I didn't need that kind of input because my own intuition was developing at a rapid pace and I was learning to listen to it more closely.

One rainy afternoon I had a reading with Linda and she told me about a class she offered that helped people open up to their psychic abilities. "It's a step-by-step, practical approach of how the skill is developed," she explained, "with a lot of emphasis on energy and how you interpret it." I decided to attend and stayed for another week.

Each day students exchanged psychic readings with each other, learning to see auras and feel subtle energies. I went home with a broader perspective of what might lie ahead of me. Following that class, this book began to grow.

I began my days with the intention of clearing my energy fields the way Linda had taught me. I visualized a white tornado engulfing my energy fields, spinning out unwanted debris into the universe to be transformed. Then I went into a quiet place and just allowed my body to feel whatever came up—a dull ache in my neck or maybe a lower back pain. I read Louise

Hay's books and tried to decipher the meaning of subtle aches and pains from the viewpoint of body language.

I was getting in touch with the subtle energies in my body and was ready for more experimenting so when a friend called to talk about Stuart Wilde and something called *The Quickening*, I decided to go.

Stuart Wilde surprised me. Here was a man who smoked, drank, and used colorful language to describe reality and the energetics within that structure. He was perfectly comfortable and at ease with himself, and had no attachment at all to what anyone thought of him. All my expectations of how a spiritual person should look, talk, and act were thrown out. Out of curiosity, and because I had never experienced the energy of someone like Stuart, I signed up for the week-long gathering called *Warrior's Wisdom: The Quickening*, in Taos, New Mexico.

That week I learned about discernment, limits, and boundaries. I was eager to learn from someone I perceived as an expert (expert because he had been at it longer than I), but I realized that another's way might not be my way.

As we sat in a meditation circle, snakes were let loose in order to teach us to stay centered and balanced and not engage in any fears about what was happening outside of ourselves. At first I was uneasy. The idea of a snake slithering around me was unnerving so I set the intention to stay centered and balanced. I kept my thoughts and emotions in alignment by placing them in a scene I created in meditation. I sat by a brook in the sun, with flowers all around and weeping willows waving in the breeze, and listened to the flowing water. When a snake touched me, I focused on expanding my experience by attempting to smell the flowers, to feel the warmth of the sun on my skin, the breeze moving through my hair. It worked because the snakes didn't worry me. It was the next experience that I couldn't deal with.

One night the group was taken into the mountains and, spaced about a hundred yards apart, told to walk into the woods by ourselves. We were to find a place to sit or stand, go into meditation, and wait until someone came to pick us up. No time frame was given and we were not to seek out or talk to anyone. If that had been all there was to it, I could have managed, but it was November in the mountains of New Mexico, snow-packed and cold; I was not prepared for the physical discomfort. Once my body got chilled, my thoughts and emotions were uncontrollable. I was not a happy camper when I was picked up four hours later. The goal was to stay balanced and centered. I failed miserably.

Then there was the firewalk—thirty feet of red-hot coals. I did it without even getting a blister. I stayed balanced and centered and felt that I had really accomplished something. Overall, the week-long experience dispelled any attachment I might have had to "spiritual significance"—the belief that some on a spiritual path develop that their mission is somehow more important than the missions of others, that they are somehow "better" than other people. This has proven to be a great gift over the years.

Sometime later, I began to date a man who had spent many years studying with Maharishi Mahesh Yogi. I learned Transcendental Meditation, or TM. It opened up a whole new realm because, up to that point, I'd had no formal instruction in meditating. I would go into what I called a contemplative state but I had a horrendous time controlling my thoughts. Every time I would reach a state of peace, a mundane thought would creep in and after a while I would become aware that I was thinking and become frustrated.

TM is simple: focus on a mantra, a word given by your instructor. It can be one or more syllables and may or may not have meaning. Every time you find that you are thinking rather than having an empty mind, you simply dispel the thought by thinking of your mantra until you return to your quiet place. This is done gently, without chastising yourself.

Later along my path, I learned to experience grace. At the time I was vice president of the Denver division of a national financial publishing company and was responsible for all aspects of the business. The most challenging part of my job was dealing with employees so I began to experiment with energy. If an employee was less than cooperative or seemed to have a lot of personal problems that interfered with his or her work, I would meditate and ask my higher self (the expanded aspect of self that is in constant contact with the soul) and the other person's higher self to come to terms with each other for the highest good of all. I would have no attachment to the outcome but would trust that it would be done. Without conscious awareness, I was practicing two important facets of *Design Your Intention*: placing my attention on an issue or situation to be resolved, and overlaying it with the intention that it would be resolved in the highest interest of all involved.

For example, I had a particular problem with a salesman who felt that he should have been promoted to my position instead of bringing in someone from outside the company to fill it. His resentment showed constantly by his antagonistic attitude toward me and the decisions I made, as well as the dissension he caused with other employees. This was compounded by a relative of his on the night shift who was involved with drugs and had to be dismissed.

Specifically, what I did was to see the situation as it existed and then how I preferred it to be. I calmed my body through breathing and went into a meditative state, using my mantra to clear my thoughts. I held the two pictures, one through my attention on the present situation and one through my intention on the result I preferred, but I would not attach any emotion to either one. As my thoughts cleared I felt a calmness permeate through all aspects of my being until I reached a point of balance and centeredness. At this point I asked my higher self to take form. That form could be anything —a ball of Light, a geometric shape, or a feeling. It rarely took the same form twice but the energy was the same and that is what I recognize and trust.

Once my higher self took form, I asked the other person's higher self to do the same. I then pulled the picture forward that I had been holding. Inwardly I asked the higher selves to come to a resolution for the highest good of all, then flooded myself with gratitude, as though it was already accomplished. It seemed to work because some days there were harmonious interactions with the salesman, but overall the strength of his resentment was too great for a complete resolution.

During this time I was also practicing gratitude to God for everything—for life, for all I had, and for everyone around me. I made this my everyday state of being for about six months, then moved into a new state of being called grace. Grace is an active path involving mental and spiritual awareness of where doors open and close and how energy is moving. It's more intellectual than the acceptance of the Path of Ease described earlier.

Being constantly grateful means living in gratitude, which is one of the aspects of grace. This allows the mind to move wherever grace takes it and to be aware of the miracles going on all around us. When experiencing grace, a blanket of ecstasy would surround me. Consciously I knew I was experiencing this new state of being. I was finely attuned to my environment and I knew ahead of time how situations were going to turn out. In business, I could intuit what printing jobs my division would get and which ones would be lost to competitors. I could also intuit potential collection problems on an account so I was prepared and able to protect the company before accepting the printing project. It was as though I couldn't make mistakes because I knew ahead of time what was happening.

Over the years, I have been able to remain in this state. Short though these ecstatic states of being are, they have begun to occur more frequently. I have also learned that when we move out of such a state, all we can do is be grateful for it and work toward reestablishing it.

My Time with Chris Griscom

Like many people, I was strongly influenced by Shirley MacLaine's books, *Out on a Limb* and *Dancing in the Light*. I was particularly fascinated by MacLaine's experience with Chris Griscom at The Light Institute in New Mexico. My fascination was with any experience that was out of what is perceived as "normal." Working with past life scenarios and opening to releasing stuck energy was not within my definition of normal so I called The Light Institute and asked for a brochure.

I called back to register for a past life workshop but it was already full. There was, however, an opening in a workshop for teachers. I told the administrator that I wasn't a teacher and he replied, "We are all teachers." With the assurance that Chris Griscom would lead some of the sessions, I signed up. I left for Galisteo, New Mexico, just outside Santa Fe.

Chris is a petite woman who radiates warmth and charm. Her style is relaxed; there is no script or plan for her workshop called *Teacher's Intensive*. As we gathered round, Chris let the energy of the group dictate what direction the lecture would take. I'm not sure how she interpreted the energy, but over the years I have come to do something similar in group gatherings.

What I learned from Chris was to let the energies gather around a group. Knowing that a specific topic will be discussed, and as the feeling of centeredness and balance with the group occurs, allow the words to begin flowing. This results in all members of the group getting the information they energetically need, and allows for a great deal of trust in your higher self. Through this workshop, I began to see the potential of letting the group as an entity set its own agenda rather than impose an agenda that did not incorporate the energy needs of a group.

A typical day began with breakfast outdoors and a meditation. Chris would lecture and then we'd take the short ride to The Light Institute for a session with a facilitator. After lunch, we'd go for a short hike, shower, and attend another lecture by Chris. Dinner was under the stars, followed by a casual conversation with Chris around the campfire.

While sitting around the fire one night I looked up and became mesmerized by lights in the sky. Could they be UFOs? My rational mind scoffed that they had to be airplanes or weather balloons or something.

Three craft hovered above the distant hills. Multicolored lights ringed a large ship while two smaller craft flitted at high speed around it. I watched them for ten minutes, until the large craft suddenly moved upward, pursued by the two smaller craft, and they all disappeared into the clouds. I had twenty hours of flight time and had passed a written test for my pilot's license so I had some knowledge of aircraft. But nothing I knew of could account for that experience. Finally I asked Chris if there were UFOs in the area. All she gave me was her famous smile. In later years, I understood that smile meant: Use your own discernment and decide for yourself what is true and what is not.

Before we left, Chris told us that the effects of the workshop would be realized in the months to come and that we should expect our lives to never again be the same. What an understatement. Shortly after I returned from the workshop, I quit my job and moved to Naples, Florida.

In Naples I continued reading and experimenting under the guidance of my higher self, but I also decided that traditional counseling would help get me in touch with an inner discomfort: blaming others for causing painful emotions. Counseling showed me that they were *my* emotions. My higher self assured me that over time I would let go of the content, or drama, and find ways to transform those feelings into energy that would enhance my life rather than hold me back.

One day I called The Light Institute and discovered they needed a business manager. The position fit with my background and personal needs so I flew to New Mexico to talk with Chris and the administrator of the Nizhoni School for Global Consciousness. I accepted the position, met with the students and teachers, explored the town, and purchased a condo—all within three days.

Over the next two years, I not only performed the duties of business manager for the school but also organized workshops and helped Chris with various other projects, including her dream of building a complete school campus. During my tenure there, I attended numerous workshops and had many sessions at The Light Institute. I was asked if I would like to train to be a facilitator but declined because I knew I could not remain dedicated to just one type of work.

During this time, my higher self assured that I would begin acquiring the tools to let go of emotional drama and transform my painful emotions into life-enhancing energy. While I was in Galisteo, I began my education of the four lower bodies—physical, emotional, mental, and spiritual—and learned to work with the four kinds of energy within them.

The physical body is the vehicle that reflects our focus within our present field of awareness. This awareness includes thoughts, feelings, and the potential of whatever our focus is. Some people approach life primarily by thinking about it, others through their emotions, and a few approach life from a "doing" point of view rather than by thinking or feeling. By observing yourself, you can tell which body you use predominantly.

The emotional body reflects the appreciation of existence. The Source-level aspects of the emotional body include appreciation, love, allowingness, true humility, and joy. When the joy of life is turned around, it's not the experience of loss that's important but how the experience is registered in the emotional body. That's why The Light Institute emphasizes emotional body work. No matter what is held in the mental or physical body, what registers in the emotional body greatly influences the others.

When the desire to create becomes manifest, the mental body of the Source itself directs that creative process. So for us, the mental body is the creative intelligence, and the emotional body fuels the creativity.

The spiritual body reflects the Source. It focuses on the essence of who we truly are so that we can see it and get in touch with it. As we balance the lower four bodies, we come to understand how they fit together and how we can use the different types of energy. Then we can touch our potential as co-creators with the Source.

Co-creatorship involves understanding the energy bodies—how they interact—and using that information to create harmony between them. When things are perceived from that state of union, a balance is created. A better way of explaining that is to perceive all energy as God. (We have chosen to categorize and separate ourselves.) By bringing our energy back and using it in a harmonious, balanced way we live in oneness with God. As we live in this oneness, we use our free will in alignment with the divine will to make choices.

For example, each day we make countless choices. If, as we ready ourselves to make a choice, we ask our higher self, "Which choice is most aligned with divine will?" we eventually will follow spirit without hesitation. This results in co-creating Heaven on Earth, a melding of our energies with the Divine.

The personality is what perceives everything as being separate. It looks at one experience and says, "It's out there," and at another and says, "It's in here." As we begin to express more and more as spirit, we come to view our experiences as being neither "out there" nor "in here" but as a journey.

The soul, being a part of spirit, wants to understand everything. It will seek that understanding physically as it expresses itself more and more in a physical structure, as well as expressing itself emotionally, mentally, and spiritually. It looks at, learns from, and assimilates whatever it sees. The soul focuses on the physical plane but because of its ability to also function on the spiritual plane, it literally acts as a transmitter.

In esoteric terms, a magnetic-attraction point from the Source allows the outreaching essence we call the soul to bring forth learning for the whole self. The radiating qualities of the soul unite the Source-level perspective with the physical-level perspective. That is why the soul is looking and looking; every level and every aspect of the self is learning from it.

Here is a sample of Chris Griscom's perspective on transforming energy from the emotional body. These are her words describing the work being done at The Light Institute. I've quoted the following information from her book *Ecstasy is a New Frequency: The Teachings of The Light Institute.* *

> We use this scenario which we call "past life" as a vehicle for touching our own self, for touching our own knowing, for looking at an experience of life and death, of love and joy, hate and fear and anger, so we can strip those away from the emotional body. Then the emotional body can quicken, can hold the frequency of the divine, at the higher octaves of energy, ecstasy, rapture.

---

* Reprinted with permission from *Ecstasy Is a New Frequency*, by Chris Griscom, Copyright 1987, Bear & Co., Santa Fe, NM.

No one ever experiences a past-life scenario that is not going on now. Our emotional bodies depict those themes, those issues, which we are still working upon, which are still within our repertoires and activating our choices now. Since our linear mind functions in time, we see scenarios in that way. We see the Middle Ages, other planets, cave men, and other historic scenarios and we call them the past. But in no way is the energy of these visions in the past; it is always our present repertoire.

To verify that, we are almost always reenacting the scenario with the same souls. Whenever we come together and have an agreement about a shared experience, we set up the play. The outcome of that play always creates a profoundly seductive energy within the emotional body to replay it again, and to replay it again with the same energy, with the same being who has been in the original repertoire...

One of the wonderful things in past-life work is that when you see your mother, your lover, your child, your boss as the bad guy or the good guy, that somebody in your movie, on an inner level, is released. So we always say, "Who is this? Is this someone you have met or known in this life?" We want to know that; it frees us from our patterning about people. Then we can let go of playing the same old game. As soon as you recognize that person, you release them and they know it. They don't have to be the pawn in your movie any more. So that person's soul, then, is released. It's wonderful, and this can be a dramatic change.

Do past-life work. Past-life work is wonderful. Do it for two reasons. One is to release yourself from this baggage that you're carrying along with you. Get rid of it.

You're not going to clear it unless you do it yourself. If somebody else reads your past lives for you, it might help you behaviorally. You might say, "Oh, that's why I feel this way about something," and it will help to some degree. But you can't clear it that way. It will just stay in your mental body, and you'll make a judgment. You'll say, "I hate that past life" or "I love that past life," which means you're still carrying around that garbage with you, and you're still on that treadmill. You want to get rid of it, even if it is a great past life. You want to move it. You want to dematerialize it into its essence form, so that the energy can come through this physical vehicle, which changes who you are in this world and what you can accomplish.

As we work with past lives, it is important to understand that our consciousness is focusing on the energetics arising from their release. That is why we pay so much attention to clearing the auric field—so that the person brings all the bodies back into a meshwork that is lighter, freer, more fluid and flexible.

The energetics are very important. We do not want people to do it in their heads. Very often in the middle of a session, a person will get a pain in the physical body, or begin to sob, because that which has been encapsulated is suddenly broken free. Sometimes the higher self will help the person pay attention, help hook that little thread from the swirling unconsciousness by using the physical body. The higher self will speak to the person through the body, e.g., there may suddenly be a pain in the right shoulder. This is a body-language cue about the burden of manifesting. The facilitator will have the person go into that part of the body and see what images are there. As those images come forth, the auric field ripples out the releasing of that encapsulation or memory, and the emotional body begins to astringe and spew. The pain may have been there for twenty lifetimes or twenty years, and it can go and never come back.

A New Experience with Energy

The syncronicity that occurs in life always amazes me. Just when I have reached completion in one area, the next in line shows up to help me move on. This happened with a woman named P. J. Deen.

A couple of months before I left Nizhoni, I was given a flyer about a local woman who taught a technique called *Awakening Your Light Body*, developed by Orin and DaBen and channeled by Sanaya Roman and Duane Packer. It wasn't her words that interested me but her picture and the energy coming from it.

The workshop consisted of three two-day sessions five weeks apart to allow us to integrate what we had experienced energetically and to give us time to practice. The first day involved a lot of meditation and I enjoyed the energies, traveling within them, and learning about energy centers in the body that were different from those I was familiar with.

Two of us had signed up, and during the first session, there seemed to something out of sync about the other participant. Nothing had been said or done to indicate that; it was just a feeling on my part. The other woman didn't show up for the second session and it soon became apparent there were good reasons for her absence and for my being the only member of the class.

The night before the second session, P. J. had been awakened by her guides. As she tells it, "They wanted me to be consciously aware of what I was about to do. I was given the image of myself going through rocks, trees, plants, and flowers and pulling out energy specifically for you so that I would be able to consciously transmit them in the form of an energy packet."

During the second session, P. J. asked for my permission to transmit the energy packet she had for me. I, of course, agreed, not really knowing what that meant. A surge of energy began to run up my legs and through my body like nothing I had ever experienced before. It wasn't uncomfortable but it wasn't like the gentle, subtle energies I was used to. After twenty or thirty minutes, P. J. began to pull away. As she did, a window started to rattle and began to close. She took it as a sign that we shouldn't stop.

The next wave of energy began to flood through me. After a while, P. J. again tried to pull away. This time not only did the window fully close, but the shutters shook as the next wave of energy was transmitted. This happened several more times. The waves of energy were strong and each had a different quality or vibration to it. Unfortunately, at the time I didn't know enough to give the waves of energy names. I can only say that one frequency was more intense, like there was more energy trying to come through. Another invoked a tingling quality within my body, whereas another made me a little nauseous. It wasn't until later work with the Light Body core group that I learned how to identify and categorize the qualities of those frequencies. Finally, we both needed to eat and were tired. With the energies still running, we ended the session.

The energies continued to flow for ten more hours. P. J. had received energy packets for others before but never before, or since, have the window and shutter moved as they did that day.

At the time, I felt that if those energies chose me to come into, then I must have a purpose in the divine plan. There was also an overwhelming feeling to stop teaching until all I said and did came from the heart rather than from the mental body.

P. J. knew her facilitating was about to move to a whole new level. It's funny because within a year, a new group signed up for *Awakening Your Light Body* with P. J. I will talk about this group later because I have only recently come in contact with them, and my experience with them so far has expanded my energy work.

Soon after the Light Body sessions, P. J. invited me to meet Linda. P. J. and Linda held individual sessions, during which time they did everything from removing implants to assisting beings of Light in helping their clients. These beings of Light would just show up as the session began. They supported in some way the individual being worked on and to my knowledge they did not have names.

P. J. and Linda invited me to join them so the three of us could work on each other. We called it "play" and met every couple of weeks to do energy work. Our meetings were great times of experimentation and I developed strong respect and trust for P. J. and Linda's abilities.

I also took a two-day channeling class, more out of curiosity than anything else. It taught me to open up to new aspects of myself. Towards the end of the class, we were asked to channel which ever being was aligning its energy with ours. I set my intention to be open to receive only the highest vibration available to me. The Lord of the Grid came through. That was the name I heard as a stream of energy communicated through me.

Regardless of the name, it became apparent about a year later on a trip to Peru (see The Ascended Masters section) why this energy aligned itself with me. It's difficult to attach too much significance to a name because it's the feeling of the energy and what that invoked within me that I found significant.

I was not prepared for the feeling of nobility and power that swept through me as the energy came forth. It was a loving energy but I was frightened because I still harbored feelings of inadequacy. For a time I refused to allow information to come forth from anything other than the higher aspects of myself. As I have grown in the realization of my oneness with All That Exists by allowing Light to penetrate my body, I have come to apply discernment to information from higher beings of Light. Discernment is simply discriminating between what you feel and think is true and what is not true for you personally.

Expanding My New Experience with Energy

I attended gatherings organized by Sanaya Roman and Duane Packer, who channel Orin and DaBen, developers of the *Awakening Your Light Body* work. After a year, I was asked if I wanted to join the core group, which had been formed two and a half years earlier, to experiment with the material before it was introduced to larger groups, often numbering as many as four hundred.

To catch up with the other members of the core group, I had to complete two and a half years of work in four months. This meant listening to fifteen volumes of tapes. Each volume consisted of sixteen tapes dealing with different subjects through guided imagery, meditation and exercise. I learned much during the year I stayed with the group, especially how to place Light into my business and everything else I did, and how to work with such vibrational frequencies as harmony, radiance, and love. Energy and/or Light pours through us in everything we do. Why not consciously place it where it's needed?

Here are two exercises from *Spiritual Growth** by Sanaya Roman. I found both of these exercises helpful. The first is *Being Your Higher Self.* This exercise assisted me feeling and strengthening the connection to my higher self, and is essential before moving into the second because the second exercise uses the higher self to assist in creating with Light.

Being Your Higher Self

The purpose of this meditation is for you to connect with that part of yourself that is your Higher Self, and to feel your Higher Self as you.

Steps:

1. Sit with your eyes open or closed. Adjust your posture so that you are comfortable, perhaps putting your hands at your sides. Begin by taking a few deep breaths.

2. Imagine your entire body relaxing, starting with your toes. Bring a feeling of relaxation into your feet, calves, and thighs, then up into your abdomen and lower back, chest, upper back, and shoulders. Next, relax your arms, hands, neck, head, and face. Let the muscles around your jaws and eyes relax. Do this until you feel peaceful, focused, and physically comfortable

3. Adjust your posture so that your energy can flow more easily up and down your spine. Breathe a full breath into just your upper chest, moving your lower diaphragm and abdomen as little as possible. Breathe into your upper chest several times; notice how you feel. Now breathe into your abdomen several times, following this with several breaths into both your upper chest and abdomen.

4. Straighten and lift your upper chest with a deep breath, so your spine is more upright. Notice that as you do this you may also want to adjust the back of your head and neck to the most comfortable upright posture. This helps create fluidity in your emotional body, open your heart center, and make it easier to think in higher ways.

5. You are now ready to meet your Higher Self. Imagine that you are being joined by many high beings who are sitting in a circle around you. Feel the peace, joy, and love all around you. These beings are here to assist you in meeting your Higher Self.

6. Imagine your Higher Self in the distance, beginning to come toward you. You might picture It as a beautiful, shimmering, radiant light. Greet and welcome your Higher Self and invite It to come closer. Mentally ask your Higher Self to assist you in making a stronger connection. Feel the radiance of Its love surrounding you and embracing you. feel the lines of light coming to you from your Higher Self. As these lines of light touch you, feel your vibration increase. Your Higher Self is now merging and becoming one with you. Feel your molecules and atoms merging with It, as if you are reclaiming a part of your energy. Let your Higher Self merge with you even more until all your energy pattern are taking on the radiance of your Higher Self. You and your Higher Self are now one.

7. As your Higher Self, open your breathing to create a greater flow of energy in your body. Adjust your posture so that you are sitting as your Higher Self. As your Higher Self, adjust your shoulders and chest to reflect your confidence and wisdom. What facial expressions do you have as your Higher Self?

8. Think of a situation you want guidance about. As your Higher Self, you are going to give yourself advice about this situation. Imagine you are a wise teacher and consultant. What advice would you give yourself on this situation? You may want to speak out loud or write down your answers.

9. As your Higher Self, do you have any other messages, perhaps about your spiritual growth, your higher purpose, or anything else?

10. Thank your Higher Self for becoming one with you and sit as long as you like as your Higher Self.

This is called the Higher Self state. You will find the more you practice this state the more you will want to think about your future and important decisions only when you are in this state. As you go into your Higher Self state, you gain the skill and ability necessary to live your life as your Higher Self.

Here is the second exercise from *Spiritual Growth** by Sanaya Roman called *Creating With Light*. This exercise that assisted me, as I mentioned earlier, to place Light into my business, my ideas, this book, and anything else I perceive as being enhanced by an infusion of Light.

Creating With Light

Steps: Get into your Higher Self state for this meditation.

1. To call light to you and charge yourself with Light:

a. Imagine making your energy as beautiful as possible. Imagining you are doing so is all that is necessary to make it beautiful. As you are making your energy beautiful, make any physical shifts in your posture that make you more comfortable, allow you to breathe deeply, and let the energy flow along your spine.

b. Take a deep breath and invite Light to come to you. Light is a living consciousness that responds instantly to your call. Let it come into your spine; imagine your spine as a rod filled with Light extending above your head and below your feet. From your spine, radiate light outward to your body. Imagine adding lines of Light throughout your body so that

---

you can hold more Light at a physical level. Send Light into
your cells, to your DNA, and then into the atoms in your
body. Completely fill you body with Light.

c. Make this Light the most beautiful color you can imagine.
What color is it? Is it a golden Light, or do you imagine a
white or bluish-white Light? Make this Light's intensity and
radiance just right for you.

d. Imagine this Light as a sphere or cocoon all around you, in
front and back, above your head and below your feet. Ex-
tend this Light beyond your body into the room. Make
your sphere of Light so large it fills the whole room or beyond. Then, make it so small it fits very close to your body.
Decide how large you want your sphere of Light that feel
just right. Does your sphere have a defined boundary, or
does it just gradually fade out? If it has a defined boundary,
where in the room does this Light stop?

2. Radiating Light:

After you have called Light to you and charged yourself
with Light, you can send Light to many different things. You
can send Light to your ideas, the future, your higher purpose,
your body, thoughts and feelings. You change the energy of
whatever you send Light to into a higher, finer vibration. Radiate Light when you are in a situation you want to change, or
send Light to other people to assist them.

a. Think of a person you want to send Light to. Start by sending Light to this person through your whole body. Notice
how it feels. Next imagine Light coming out of your eyes,
hands, or heart and going directly to this person. Use the
way of sending Light to others that feels the most comfortable and right to you.

b. Think of something you want to send Light to. Call Light to
you and charge yourself with Light. Imagine yourself being
as clear as a crystal, so that you are a pure transmitter of
Light. Then, send Light to whatever you have chosen. Next,
send energy through your heart and then through your
whole body to this thing. Using the way of sending Light
that feels the most comfortable and right to you.

c. Think of other things you want to send Light to, such as world peace, the earth, animals or whatever you like. Notice that as you send Light your own Light becomes brighter and more beautiful.

d. You have now learned how to call Light to you, charge yourself with Light, and radiate Light.

The Ascended Masters

During my work with Sanaya Roman, I discovered *The "I AM" Discourses*, a multi-volume work channeled by Godfre Ray King in the 1930s from Ascended Master St. Germain. The material gave me information about the Spiritual Hierarchy of this universe and inspired me to read everything I could find about the Ascended Masters.

When the time came to leave Sanaya and Duane's Light Body gatherings, my "play" sessions with P. J. and Linda were also coming to an end. It was then that Linda introduced me to a most remarkable woman in Albuquerque: Dr. Norma Milanovich.

Dr. Milanovich holds a Masters and a Doctorate degree from the University of Houston, is president of a training and development corporation, and has transmitted to the United Nations Parapsychology Society a message from Master Kuthumi of the Spiritual Hierarchy.

She has also co-authored *We, the Arcturians,* information from the fifth-dimensional beings she was channeling before the Ascended Masters assumed the task of transmitting through her.

My first encounter with Norma occurred when I visited her for a reading from the Ascended Masters. Kuthumi came through from the seventh dimension and spoke. Then St. Germain came through and asked if I would be a Keeper of the Flame.

I was already invoking the Violet Flame (which transforms and transmutes low frequency energy such as fear and hate), combining it with the white Light of the tornado that I call down to clear my energy field. He said I would have to determine for myself what being a "Keeper" meant and requested me to formally accept the designation. He briefly described a ceremony of acceptance which I later performed. My feeling is that anyone who uses the Violet Flame with dedication, and lives in integrity with their code of life is a Keeper of the Flame.

There is a guided meditation that has really helped me to enhance the flow of energy through the energycenters within the physical body called chakras, It is done with the assistance of the Ascended Masters. This meditation is from one of Norma's workshops called *Understanding the Celestial Realms and Working with the Ascended Masters.* *

First, let's review the location of the chakras from the bottom up:

> *The first chakra (or root chakra) is located at the base of the spine.*
>
> *The second chakra (or the seat of the soul chakra) is located about three inches above the sexual organs.*
>
> *The third chakra (or solar plexus chakra) is located in the area of the navel.*
>
> *The fourth chakra (or heart chakra) is located in the area of the heart.*
>
> *The fifth chakra (or throat chakra) is located in the area of the throat.*
>
> *The sixth chakra or third eye chakra is located between the eye brows, at the center of the forehead.*
>
> *The seventh chakra or crown chakra is located in the center of the top of the head, and is usually associated with the pituitary gland.*

---

*   *Understanding the Celestial Realms and Working with the Ascended Masters,*
      © 1994 by Dr. Norma Milanovich. Reprinted by permission of Athena Publishing.

Understanding the Celestial Realms and Working with the Ascended Masters

Sit in a comfortable chair and relax. Breathe deeply, bringing in prana. Focus your attention on your chest, your heart and your back. Feel any tension there and let it go. See it drift off into the universe. Focus your attention on your head, your neck, your shoulders. Feel any tension and let it go. Breathe deeply and feel your body relax. Visualize every cell ready to receive the white Light.

As you sit perfectly relaxed, begin to move into a field. See the flowers. Smell the greenery. Feel the fresh air brush across your face. Notice the radiance of the golden sun as it falls down around your shoulders.

Look across the field. Notice there is a master standing there. As he walks forward, you notice he is carrying in his hands a beautiful red ball. It is a crimson ball and he offers it to you. You take it in both of your hands and thank him. The master is Archangel Michael and he has come forward to assist you on your journey. Place the crimson red ball at the base of your spine. Spin it faster and faster, then fleck it with Light, like Light you would see coming from a beautiful crystal. Move it to the left and move it to the right. Feel it cleansing and purifying the lower chakra. Feel its strength as it is grounding you to the earth.

Then look up. There is another master in the distance, walking forward. As he walks forward, you see that he is carrying in his hands an orange ball of Light. It is Master Kuthumi. He has a beautiful smile on his face as he approaches you, and he hands you this orange ball of light. Bless it and tell him thank you, as you accept it. Spin it in your hands and see the Light flecks all the way through it. Place it in your abdomen. Move it to the left and move it to the right as it is spinning. Feel its energy.

As you look up, you notice there is another master in the distance. It is Lady Nada. She comes to you with a yellow ball of energy in her hands. She approaches you and bows. She offers you this yellow ball of energy. Tell her thank you. Accept it and spin it and fleck it with Light. See how fast it spins. Place it in your solar plexus. Feel its energy moving to the left and moving to the right, purifying you and making you strong.

Then look up and notice that Sanada is coming forward and in his hands he has a beautiful green ball of energy representing the heart. As he comes forward he offers you this ball of energy. Tell him thank you and feel the love from your heart as you accept this green ball of energy. Spin it in your hands and fleck it once again with the Light of a beautiful crystal. Place it in your heart center and move it to the left and to the right. Feel its energy as it moves forward and backward. Feel the strength in your heart and the love flowing because it is placed there.

Looking up once again, you see Master El Morya is coming forward with a blue ball of energy. He says he is so pleased to serve you. Tell him thank you and accept the blue ball of energy. Spin it in your hands and fleck it with crystal Light. Place it in your throat center and feel the courage and the strength of communication come forward. Feel how good it feels as it moves to the left and to the right.

You now see Lady Isis coming forward and in her hands is a beautiful indigo ball of energy. She approaches you and hands you this indigo ball of prophets' visions. Thank her and feel the energy in your hands. Spin the ball, fleck it with Light and place it within your third-eye area. Have it move to the left and to the right, spinning faster and faster.

Now the mighty St. Germain comes forward. In his hands is a beautiful violet frequency, a violet ball of energy. He approaches you and offers you this gift. Take the violet ball, spin it in your hands, fleck it with crystal Light and feel its energy radiating in your hands. Place it on your crown chakra and feel the violet frequency moving to the left and to the right as it is spinning faster and faster. Then feel this energy penetrating your entire aura as it moves down to your feet. Feel the protection and feel any negativity dissolving.

Look down from the violet and see it being supported by the indigo. Look below that and see the blue band, then the green, then the yellow band below that, the orange below that, and the mighty strength of the red. See all these mighty colors in perfect balance and feel them turning into the white Light. Feel them radiate from your cells, down through the bottom of your feet, up through your crown chakra. Feel the power of this white Light as your aura is expanded way beyond the boundaries of the room. Feel that energy. Staying totally relaxed, breath deeply and, in this perfect state of mind, say the following:

I am a radiant being of Light and love.
I am a radiant being of Light and love.
I am a radiant being of Light and love.

Miracles happen wherever I go.
Miracles happen wherever I go.
Miracles happen wherever I go.

All that I need comes to me easily.
All that I need comes to me easily.
All that I need comes to me easily.

My health and body are perfect, they are stronger every day.
My health and body are perfect, they are stronger every day.
My health and body are perfect, they are stronger every day.

I complete all my work perfectly, quickly, easily and effortlessly.
I complete all my work perfectly, quickly, easily and effortlessly.
I complete all my work perfectly, quickly, easily and effortlessly.

Abundance comes to me effortlessly and I am grateful and I deserve it.
Abundance comes to me effortlessly and I am grateful and I deserve it.
Abundance comes to me effortlessly and I am grateful and I deserve it.

Breathe deeply. Move the prana through yourself. Visualize the support of the Ascended Masters and the seven colors that you command. These are perfect frequencies that you have placed, with the Ascended Masters' help, in your chakra system. They are balanced and they are impenetrable. You are the white Light.

If you feel any tension in your body, let it go. Take command. Feel your body respond to the Light and to your emotions. Feel your breath, the prana, for this is your real state of beingness, this is your power.

Now focus on your heart center, the key to your destiny. See the seven glorious masters standing around you like pillars of Light. Feel their radiance. Open your crown chakra to the Great Central Sun. Connect all the way up through the causal plane, the gateway to the Great Central Sun's golden energy. Feel it come all the way down through your crown chakra, penetrating the white Light moving down through your feet, all the way down to the core of Mother Earth. Feel your power as you are the link of Lights to the heavens and to the Earth. You are now connected to the Great Central Sun. Feel the energy of it come down, and as your aura increases, feel how its love touches you. Nothing that is less than this vibrational frequency can harm you or touch you. This is your perfect Light. Everything else is an illusion.

Coming back now through the stellar gateway, back through your seven chakras and the white Light, all perfectly balanced. Thank the Ascended Masters through your own higher self for working with you today. Once again, you are in the field. Smell the roses and the flowers, feel the coolness in the air. You are now back in the third-dimensional world, feeling empowered and balanced.

Norma also co-authored *Sacred Journey to Atlantis,* a book about a journey she organized to Bimini where, it is said, part of Atlantis is still under water. Norma organizes trips to perform specific energy work to aid the planet and humanity, usually involving the planetary grid system.

The electromagnetic planetary grid system is a web of Light that encircles Earth. The frequency and intensity of that Light depend on the level of humanity's consciousness. In other words, each one of us holds the power to affect the vibrations of Earth's grid of Light.

My first trip with Norma was with a group going to Bolivia and Peru with the goal of raising our own frequencies, thereby affecting the grid, raising the frequency of every human on Earth, and shifting the mass consciousness to bring to Earth the divine plan of the Source: oneness and love.

At Machu Picchu, I sensed I was working on behalf of the devic kingdom. (Devas are the elemental spirits associated with nature, especially plants and animals.) Then I remembered that P. J. had told me that the energy packet she'd given me had contained energy from plants, trees, rocks, and flowers. This confirmed that everything I had experienced in the past had happened for a purpose and would one day prove useful.

Norma also arranged trips to Israel, Maui, Tibet, China, the North Pole, India, and Africa. When I felt guided to go physically, I'd go; otherwise, I connected with the group energetically and work from wherever I was.

Another association I have with Norma is through Trinity Foundation, a nonprofit organization she organized. The foundation has a governing board called the Council of Twelve on which I served. Each seat is held for a minimum of one year, and after a year, I was guided to release my position so I would be available for other work that was being assigned to me. (An aspect of myself still contributed to the Council on an energy level.)

The foundation's purpose is designed to serve humanity in its transition into the fifth dimension. One way is through the building of a structure called the Templar. As individuals walk through this structure, their frequencies will increase.

For information on the Trinity Foundation or any of Norma's other work, which includes speaking engagements, videos, seminars, tapes, books, trips, and newsletters, please contact her directly at the address in the Resources section.

Brian Grattan and Janet McClure

When I received the guidance to let go of my position with the Trinity Foundation, a new level of information began coming in and a new teacher appeared in my life. His name was Brian Grattan.

Brian died following a seminar in Basel, Switzerland, in 1995. He had been in pain since the beginning of the week and I didn't feel he would be with us much longer, but I had no idea it would happen as fast as it did.

I had read Brian's book, *Mahatma,* a few years earlier and it had stretched my perception of reality. The material was difficult at first because it was clouded with personality issues, but I found that the quality of information far outweighed anything else.

Two words in particular need to be defined: Source and Mahatma. Source is the term Brian used to describe what most of us refer to as God, All That Is, the Creator. Mahatma is the mantra used to invoke all the energies of self that exist from here to the Source. A combination of these self energies is referred to as the I AM Presence. The energy of the I AM Presence is from the self in existence in the physical body to the Self in existence at the Source. Mahatma encompasses all that and more.

Brian believed that the I AM Presence consisted of 352 levels unified from Earth to the Source. These levels exist within a total of nine dimensions and each of the 352 levels contains aspects of ourselves that already exist but of which we are unaware. Embracing the awareness of each of these levels is called self-realization, and we do this through accepting Light into our bodies.

Another of Brian's theories is that as the Source individualized, it differentiated itself into a structure from which to create. This structure consists of twelve rays and the combination of these rays make up the Source. Each ray has a quality within its frequency band of energy and has a color associated with it.

For example, the first ray is Divine Will and the associated color is red. The second ray is Love-Wisdom, which is blue. The third ray is Active Intelligence and is yellow, and so on. According to Brian, beyond the tenth ray something called the spiritual microtron is available to us. Through the fusion of the atom and the microtron, we begin to integrate the spiritualization of matter. The energy of this fusion is absorbed by the atom and the microtron fields within the physical body. These Rays have an intricate connection to the chakra system, the study of which is complex.

I attended many of Brian's workshops and received a combination of esoteric and practical information. The workshops included a lot of meditation, which allowed me to receive the energy and come to my own conclusions without a lot of verbal explanation. This is always based on a person's level of consciousness: another reason to be discerning.

I studied Brian's perceptions of and ideas about the Source with great interest. I mentioned a few with the hopes that Brian's work will find an ever-widening audience. I had already been introduced to some of Brian's information because of the work of the late Janet McClure. (Her channelings can be acquired through the New Tibetans, formerly the Tibetan Foundation.) Janet had been one of Brian's sources so I imagine he combined her information with the information he received inwardly to come up with his own theory of creation.

Because I perceive channeling as a means of acquiring information from beyond our present perceptions, a brief review might be in order. Channeling has been around since the beginning of humanity yet it is often misunderstood. The most accepted form of channeling is the information on which religions are based. Let me explain. A voice is heard, which is assumed to be God or the Holy Spirit. For example, the Koran is said to have been dictated to Mohammed by God. Others who have received the word of God include Moses, Abraham, and Mary. Some write what they hear, others say what they hear, while still others are inspired to produce art or music.

Channeling encompasses the receiving of energy or information from beyond one's self and using it in some way. There are two types of channeling: conscious and trance. In conscious channeling, the channeler knows all that occurs during the channeling, whereas in trance channeling, the channel is consciously absent and has no recall of the communication.

A discussion on channeling must include the chakras because chakras are nexus points for energy. It is important that all seven chakras are integrated. Before trying to channel, you might want to ask each chakra, "What do you think of integration? Do you understand it? Do you allow it? Do you trust it?"

Based on how each of the seven chakras reply, do whatever releasing, transmuting or transforming is needed. Look at the patterns that need to be changed and then direct into that chakra the energy of the Violet Flame. Chakras are linked to particular points of awareness within you. Be flexible about understanding the specifics.

Channeling emphasizes integration. It makes apparent the ever-changing, ever-evolving effects of integration. By using your channel, you become your own connection to the evolutionary process. You narrow and stabilize that process by being in the body. The physical body has been created as a focal point for stabilizing the creative process of the Source. Think of yourself as a channel, one who molds the creative process into a viewing-response system. Channeling pure energy is a tool given to us by the Source to allow the divine plan to evolve.

The following four exercises can assist you in beginning the channeling process. The meditation is from a series of twelve lessons channeled by Janet McClure from her book *Channeling Insights*.*

Channeling Insights

See yourself standing in the center of a large circle and as you do, a golden Light encases the physical structure. Allow it to penetrate deeply into your physical structure. Deeper and deeper and deeper. As it penetrates to the cellular or atomic level, sense golden radiation coming from that level and flowing out to the perimeter of this circle. The perimeter of the

* *Channeling Insights*, Tibetan Foundation, Inc., 1987. Reprinted by permission.

circle begins to glow and to respond vibrationally, to reflect back to you again the golden Light. All around you this radiant golden Light comes in again to your physical structure. You then allow this new level of radiance to penetrate to the atomic level, setting up a flow which then again goes out or radiates to the perimeter of the circle.

Please stay within this visualization for about ten minutes. Try to get to the point where all radiation is simultaneous and not sequential, and then see what occurs to you. Dismiss, after ten minutes, the imagery as given and go into your own meditative state from it. I invite you to then remain for as long as you wish within this meditation. When you return, jot down a summary, a brief one, of what occurred. You are then to do this meditation for the next two weeks. At the end of that time, look over your notes and integrate into your understanding what has occurred through them.

After completing the above exercise for two weeks, you will have reached a level of comfort and competence in your ability. I feel the next exercise called *Stepping on Light,* channeled by Janet McClure from the book *Light Techniques that Trigger Transformation** by Vywammus, will help expand your ability.

Stepping on Light

View yourself walking on a path of Light. We could say it is a road that is lit up.

It is transparent but what you see through it is simply more Light, so it is an intense Light that you are walking on. As you walk on it, the Light isn't solid, so you sink into the Light. Now, it seems very supportive, even if you are sometimes knee deep in Light. Sometimes you don't sink in that much. You can begin to dance on this Light—whatever kind of dance you wish. Begin to dance on it. Now you will note something interesting. If you turn around and look at the path where you have been, you have left footprints there, footprints in the Light, and you know that your unique footprints are a permanent

* *Light Techniques that Trigger Transformation,* Light Technology Publishing, 1989.

part now of that Light. You've changed the Light by stepping on it. What you are has created a difference in the Light, not in an inappropriate sense, but your footprints, or your dance, has now become part of what that Light is.

Now, of course, you recognize that the footprints of everyone that has ever been and ever will be walking in the Light blend. And if you look closely, you will see coming toward you someone else on that Light path, and their footprints sometimes enlarge your footprints, creating a unique pattern in the Light that is beyond what either one of you could create. Your footprints have now joined to create a unique interpretation of Light expression. The little one comes up to you and asks you to dance and the two of you continue down the path dancing together, creating unique footprints together—a cosmic Light dance indeed.

View, then, a much larger road that all humanity dances on. It is a Light path right here on the physical plane. All of humanity is dancing together on it. Can you dance on a path of Light if you are not yet aware of yourself as Light? Of course. There are levels of self that are aware of it in everyone. Thus, we are talking about a cosmic dance in which the soul level participates fully, willingly and creatively.

However, on the physical plane your permission is needed to grow in awareness of how to use the physical plane's expression in a more comprehensive manner. In other words, your physical point of view must willingly allow itself to recognize Light. When it does so, the path that is physical joins the path that is spiritual. The coming together unites and expands the path. It becomes a very cosmic perspective and yet the focus of it, for a while anyway, remains physical. It takes with it eternally what has been gained on the physical plane. The cosmic dance of Light is chosen by all aspects of self, allowing the footprints to reflect an awareness that Light is an interaction of creative possibilities with all levels, all aspects, all potentialities. The more that is realized, the Lighter the path, the more comprehensively one dances, the greater the perspective of Light comes forth.

Here is another exercise from the book *Light Techniques that Trigger Transformation** by Vywammus, channeled through Janet McClure. This exercise is important because it gives you the tools to learn from the perspective you've chosen in any given situation.

Energizing Goals By Breaking Up Crystallized Patterns

See yourself walking down a corridor. There are doors on both sides of the corridor and as you walk, you know you are going to make choices. You will walk to a particular door and open it. Note if it is on the right or left. Go to that particular door.

Now the goal is to learn from the perspective you've chosen. There will be a symbolic experience that you will gain by going through this door but first of all, before you open the door, as you stand there before it, through your third eye project Light right through the door because Light is not stopped by a door. Project Light through the door as much as you can. Sense Light flooding into that symbolic experience that you are about to enter. Allow about two minutes of projection here; you might want to use a clock to show you that at least two minutes have gone by. Spend two minutes projecting the Light into this experience and then open the door. You will have a symbolic experience which you will interpret much as you do a dream, using the same sort of symbology.

Remember that if you see other people in connection with your experience, one way to interpret that is to see all people as a part of yourself. In this experience, however, because it is a Light-projection experience, other people may also represent other parts of the plan or other people as they interact with you. Thus it will be necessary to interpret from several points of view—from a holistic point of view where you play all of the roles in this symbolic experience.

This technique will improve your ability to interpret what is going on in your life beyond what you consciously recognize

* *Light Techniques that Trigger Transformation*, Light Technology Publishing, 1989.

at this point, and also your ability to see into your relationships with others. Projecting Light into an opportunity will Light up that opportunity and energize it with Light that has a magnetic attraction. I would suggest, then, as a progression of this exercise, that whenever you know very clearly what you want in your life—and I say that very carefully—that you stand before the door to it and project Light through the door into that opportunity to energize it before you enter into a relationship with it.

For example, you may seek full abundance. It is important, however, to know what sort of resistance you hold against abundance. Unless you are currently allowing an unlimited flow, right now you do have some resistance, and it is important to discover what it is and why it is there to avoid energizing the resistance.

Now, does that mean that you shouldn't use this technique? Of course not. But it can mean that you should not overuse the technique. Two minutes is about the right length of time. Twenty or thirty minutes of projecting Light into an opportunity may put so much energy into the resistance part that you will have greater difficulty in connecting with the goal than if you hadn't done the exercise at all.

This last exercise from *Light Techniques that Trigger Transformation** has been added to assist in the integration process.

Electrical Stimulation of Integration

See a large circle before you. It is horizontal. You are sitting just outside the circle. You could sit within it but you are not. There are ten vertical pillars placed within the circle, wherever you wish to see them. They are silver metal cylinders, electrical in nature. There is an electrical stimulative point within the circle, and the circle simply represents a whole point of view, whether it is your whole life, the Source's whole existence, a day that is a whole perspective in your life, a book that has been written and is complete—anything that is complete at a

---

* *Light Techniques that Trigger Transformation*, Light Technology Publishing, 1989.

level, the circle represents. So it really represents a coming together, an integration of a particular perspective.

Now create through your third eye a beam of Light and have it focus on the whole circle. It will connect into the ten silver rods, and you will begin to sense the energy that is being stored within them. Energize them until you know they are very vibrant indeed. It will probably take, again, around two minutes. Now, this energy is very vibrant; it does not destroy, it simply stimulates. I want you now to go into the circle. Become the right size for what you've visualized so that you can move easily among these cylinders, touching one and then swinging to another. As you let go of one you grab hold of another. There is a way of continuing to hold on to one and then grasping another as you let go of the first one. Now you can continue to move from one to another until you have covered all ten of them, and then you can go through them again. There is no need to stop your flow. As you move from one to another you are energized by them. It might equate to a mild electric shock but it is simply stimulative and each one is stimulating you in a slightly different way.

Now as you move from one to another, sense that each one prods your consciousness a little, prods the mental processes so that you can think more clearly, prods your spiritual knowingness so that you can connect more completely, prods your emotional body so that you can flow more completely, and prods your physical responses so they may respond more completely. Sense, then, the stimulation as you swing from rod to rod. Do this for three or four moments. Then you may need to go back and energize the rods again for another minute or two, after which you can go back and move again among the rods.

Now this is an integrative exercise, allowing stimulus but movement, allowing movement but balance, allowing balance but the ability to progress a connection through stimulation. In this manner we begin to see, literally, the integrative possibilities of all of what, up until this point, has seemed stuck in the third dimension, seems crystallized into the third dimension, seems resistive within the third dimension. You begin then to dimensionalize the physical experience in a way that you

haven't recognized before. You can direct a consistent relationship with the dimensions through such an exercise. You
can allow the four bodies to really gain a perspective on all of
the available physical dimensions.

Sometimes the difficulty on the physical plane is that certain dimensions have been skipped over by certain parts of
your consciousness. Through this exercise of stimulating all ten
points, you are really entering the third, fourth, and fifth dimensions, with some reflection of the sixth dimension and
allowing a progressive lighting up which releases, in rather an
intricate way, certain points resistive to the use of some of the
dimensional focuses. Again, it is very good to allow a complete
flowing dimensionally as the points of contact are made that
bridge any particular gaps in a dimensional understanding. You
get caught in the gaps and have difficulty bridging, so this
technique will begin to sort out the means to allow the four-
body system to express in the full dimensional experience. The
Light flows, of course, on all dimensional levels; thus, the bridge
is the Light, which then allows your energy to cross it easily
and without resistance. It allows you to be aware of the conti-
nuity of the flow, of the integrative possibilities of your life.

Angels

A year prior to Brian's passing, I was guided to let go of all
attachments to people or objects considered to be teachers on
any level. This meant looking at Brian differently. I had to stay
within my power and not give it away. When we look upon
someone or something as being greater than us, we actually
give away part of our power. I had already been fairly conscious
about holding my power, so I suspected that the guidance was
also letting me know I would soon desire no input from outside myself, and if I chose to join a group, it would only be to
assist Earth and humanity in their evolution.

Even if at the time I don't clearly understand the reasons, I
always take my guidance seriously. When Brian left the physical plane I missed someone I liked and respected, but I did not

feel lost as so many did. Their attachment to Brian and what he represented left them feeling insignificant without him.

After returning from Basel, I decided to take a few months off to contemplate and meditate. It proved to be both rewarding and painful. Without the constant rush of planning one event after another, I was forced to face levels of deep resistance in regard to owning my own power completely, and to openly and publicly own my beliefs. I feared the inadequacy of offering my viewpoint to others by teaching or facilitating energy. By looking at my resistance I was able to embrace it as another aspect of my wholeness. I concluded that we never get rid of anything. The whole point of life is to transmute fear and allow love to replace it.

In the beginning of my work with Brian, angels began to appear in my reality. I felt their presence and they would communicate with me during meditation, I often saw a mist of color and heard a voice telling me which angel was communicating with me. This happened so often that I wrote a guided meditation to invoke the assistance of specific archangels and other celestial energies to help move me through the dimensions so I could experience them. I know there have been times when my inner nudge or guidance has come from the angelic realms because of how it feels while I'm getting the information.

I have come to know that the energy I call Archangel Michael stands as a pillar through my essence and that I have been connected throughout all my lifetimes with this energy. (The energy I refer to as Archangel Michael is not the energy of an individual but the energy of an office within the Source. We often label energies with specific names and gender when a more accurate description would be a name defining their particular duty within the divine plan.)

Through my connection with the angelic realms I have a more complete understanding of the beings that guide planet Earth, including angels and archangels who can easily penetrate all the dimensions so they can function throughout creation.

Here is the guided meditation I wrote about angels, based on the information I learned from Brian. As with any of meditations or exercises that are lengthy, it might prove beneficial to tape them. It's much easier to experience a guided meditation or exercise while listening to it rather than reading it.

The Multi-dimensional Meditation

I begin with the following invocation:

> Great Presence of Life flowing through the undifferentiated Source, the Mahatma, my mighty I AM Presence, any Archangels, Angels and Ascended Masters destined to work with me, I ask for assistance so that all aspects of self throughout eternity and in all alternate realities from here to the undifferentiated Source now come into alignment to be recognized as the oneness that I AM. With this assistance, I invoke a white/violet tornado representing the white energy of Source and the violet energy of transmutation to transform any resistance within my four bodies so that I may begin.

I visualize a gold and white thread of Light from the Source to my crown chakra. Once this visualization is clear I continue to widen this thread until it becomes a channel of gold and white Light so that my four-body system is included within it. The gold encompasses the colors of all the rays, and the Mahatma energy and the incandescent white is the energy of the Source.

When this feels completed, I ask specific archangels for their assistance so that I may receive this energy fully into my body. Khamael, Tzaphkiel, Tzadkiel, Ratziel, Michael, Auriel, Raphael and Gabriel, each knowing the area of the body, can assist with most effectively. I then call upon Metatron for all he can do so that I do not limit his assistance, and Sandalphon who I ask to assist me in anchoring this energy into the Earth.

Then I ask Metatron and Sandalphon to connect so that, through their connection, I may be assisted with the integration, any transmutation needed, and the exchange with the Earth for what it wants to use, and for what I want to receive from the Earth.

Breathing deeply for a moment, allowing any resistance to be burned in the transformational fire of the violet energy, I invite the energy of the aqua-colored microtron that has been anchored into the Earth to come up and merge with the golden/white Light, blending into a golden/white/aqua-colored flow, moving continuously throughout my entire four bodies until this energy encompasses all within my channel back to the undifferentiated Source.

Once this energy has reached the undifferentiated Source, I visualize it traversing from the Source to the Earth, back and forth, encompassing all of me and speeding up until there is no beginning and no end that can be felt or seen. There is just a continuous motion cycling from Source to Earth, up and down, in and out within my channel, throughout all my bodies. Once again, I call upon the assistance of all beings who are present to aid in perfecting this exercise, taking a few moments now for that assistance.

Feeling the golden/white/aqua Light flow throughout my bodies, I invoke perfect health, right livelihood, and right alignment with Divine Will. I invoke the alignment of myself with All That Is, my own I AM Presence, and Mahatma. I continue to open myself to receive Mahatma and give thanks for the abundance in my life.

By consciously breathing out more and more into the Light as Light, I move through the dimensional levels acknowledging that I AM one with each level. I now expand through the Universal Levels to the sixth dimension. I meet a great being and ask for his assistance to help me integrate all of the Universal levels before moving into the seventh dimension. In order to integrate all Universal levels, I am instructed to see myself as this great being and he/she as I. At this point I am ready to move into the seventh dimension.

This great being that I am one with shows me a golden bridge leading to the monadic levels, which are the dimensions beyond this one. Breathing deeply, I call upon the violet energy to transform any resistance I may have that would keep me from crossing the bridge. Once I have crossed, I feel nothing but contentment and bliss. I am greeted by many and am one with all. The Mahatma energy now introduces me to another great being. As I bathe in the radiance of this great one's presence, I breathe in more fully my co-creator consciousness as one with All That Is.

I now embody this great being and allow the Mahatma energy to take me through the balance of the seventh dimension, then the eighth dimension, forever expanding my consciousness as I recognize that this is also who I AM. The Mahatma then guides me as the Mahatma into the ninth dimension where I witness an oval table. Around this table are seated the most wondrous beings, radiant in Divine Light and Love. There are no words to express the ecstasy and bliss that I AM. As I look into the eyes of these great ones who are the twelve Rays that, when combined, make up the Source, I see my own reflection and realize that I AM them and they are me and there is no separation. Radiating into their omnipresence and knowing without any doubt that this is who I AM, I stay within this conscious level of awareness and know that there will never again be a sense of finite limitation and if there is, I will concentrate on my Source channel and surrender to my I AM Presence.

I am no longer without control of my reality. I surrender to the I AM of my I AM Presence. I shall never again feel less than. I AM a multidimensional being. I will continue to become the Mahatma. I refuse to ever give my power to anyone, other than my own I AM. I will continue to love, to create, and to live an abundant, joyful life within the framework of the greater I AM. I see totally through the illusion of that which I have always held to be my total reality. I realize now that the totality of who I am is connected, that all levels of self are now and always were united.

Moving back through the levels of the ninth dimension, still vibrating from the radiation of the omnipresence of the twelve Rays making up the differentiated Source, moving through the levels of the eighth dimension, I continue on through the seventh dimension until I come once again to the golden bridge. Before crossing I visualize the radiance I am now reflecting to be placed into the physical/universal dimensions

I am about to enter. I also visualize this radiance throughout all the cells in my body, seeing the gold which encompasses all Rays and the incandescent white Light of Source energy as one unified field. This energy permeates throughout all that I know to be myself, shimmering like a curtain that dances, permeating all within and without, all cells, all bodies for I have crossed and I am now in my physical dimension.

Taking some deep breaths, I say to myself, "I am divine Light and love. I am complete as my own I AM of my I AM Presence. I recognize now that I have always been the I AM. I glory and revel in the Light and the love." I breathe in the incandescent white Light of Source, as my developing channel becomes that Light. I am able to sense colors and sounds that I have never before been able to experience.

I am now able to experience this part of myself, which is the I AM Presence. I AM a child of the Light. I love the Light. I serve the Light. I live in the Light, I am protected, illuminated, and sustained by the Light and I bless the Light.

Coming Out of Hibernation

Seven months had passed since Brian's death. I began to notice an inner nudge telling me to attend a gathering in Hawaii that a group from Santa Fe was organizing. I was astonished to discover that they were the very individuals who had taken the Awakening Your Light Body course a year after I did. There are no accidents but the syncronicity of events still amazes me. The name of this group is Circle of Divine Unity.

I stayed on the fringe of the gathering and spent most of my time observing rather than participating. I had difficulty staying focused, perhaps because I had never before experienced a group of people who process so openly. (Processing is the integration into the physical body of a realization or a point of Light. It can take the form of tears, uncontrollable laughter, or shakes and jerks as the body adjusts to new energy and releases resistance.) I left, not knowing if this was a path I wanted to pursue.

A new year rolled around and I felt it was time for teaching from the heart to come forward. I had been guided that I had the first six months of the year to gather the information I needed, including information on sacred geometry. I was to find a source for that information that would satisfy my mental body.

The Flower of Life workshops appeared to be the source of the information I needed so I signed up for a workshop in San Francisco. Some of the information in this workshop included the Ancient Egyptian Mystery School teachings, the ascension process, understanding dimensional shifts, the history of planet Earth with explanations about Atlantis and Lemuria, and a how to connect and merge with the higher Self.

Before attending the workshop, however, I had a strong urge to go to the Wesak Festival on Mt. Shasta. Wesak is considered by the Ascended Masters to be the holiest day of the year, the time of the most intense pouring down of spiritual energy.

When two or more people gather together for a purpose, they form what is called "a group vehicle," a vehicle of energy that can be used to explore aspects of the Source vaster than those available to an individual. I go to gatherings to tap into the energy created by a group vehicle. The Wesak Festival is an excellent opportunity to create a strong group vehicle because more than 1200 people attend. The group can use this energy for personal intention as well as for the group intention of accelerating the evolution of Earth, humanity, and all the rest of creation.

Observing so many people was a wonderful experience. Even if there are some people we dislike, it is important to remember that the stream of energy beneath the exterior facade is the same: we all desire, consciously or unconsciously, to help the divine plan to manifest.

Another good reason to attend Wesak Festival is to experience the invocations and activations called forth by Dr. Joshua David Stone. Among the most powerful I have experienced, they continue to work for months after the celebration.

The group vehicle created in such gatherings offers a means one can use until we can access the energy on our own. Group intent, invocation, and focus brings through the omnipresence of pure love, that we might be fed the nectar of the Source. It has given me the opportunity to anchor pure Creator levels of consciousness into my teaching and facilitating; in return, I offer it to any who attends my gatherings.

Finally, the day came for the San Francisco Flower of Life workshop. There was pressure to get everything in order as I'd been guided to do. Often it is easy to put off doing something we've been guided to do because of everyday life, work, and family. I could no longer use those excuses.

The workshop was intense. Drunvalo Melchizedek received a lot of his information from Thoth, the Egyptian god of wisdom, and from the angelic realm. Drunvalo calls this information the Teaching of the Right Eye of Horus and is a left-brained perspective of creation. The Flower of Life teachings place everything in a wave-form universe that uses the language of Light and sound.

Everything within a wave-form universe is contained within the geometry of the Flower of Life. The geometry of this shape is nineteen interconnecting circles and the Flower of Life symbol can be found on the walls of ancient ruins all over the world. Drunvalo guided us through the information he received from Thoth, taking us from before the great pyramid was built to the time of Lemuria and Atlantis. The creation and downfall of these two civilizations and how a few survivors scattered around the world and began civilizations mystifies us even today. The Egyptian civilization is one of those civilizations built by Atlantean survivors.

According to the teachings, Thoth chose Egypt, and built the great pyramid in an attempt to heal the dimensional tear created by the destruction of the Atlantean civilization. The great pyramid and other structures throughout Egypt have other functions; within the geometry of the architecture, energy vortexes were created so an individual could access different dimensions. This was an initiation and before being allowed to enter these areas, the initiate had to pass certain tests. The pass-

ing of these tests moved initiates through the ascension process, ascending to the next level.

Within the symbol of the Flower of Life is the geometric
image of Light and sound. Anything within a wave-form universe can be broken down to its geometric formula and then be
found within the Flower of Life symbol.

The finale of the workshop was the Christ Consciousness
Spherical Breathing technique, which is suppose to assist an
individual to experience—and eventually physically move
into—the fourth dimension. I will share this technique with
you with a word of warning. If it is practiced regularly, I strongly
recommend attending a workshop to establish a foundation
because there are many levels to the Flower of Life.

The Christ-Consciousness Spherical Breathing technique
came to Drunvalo Melchizedek from the angelic realms. He
then trained facilitators to present this and his other information in the Flower of Life workshops. The facilitator of the
workshop I took was Bob Frissell; because of the complexity of
this material, I have relied on the explanations of this technique from Bob's book, *Nothing in This Book Is True, but It's
Exactly How Things Are.**

The Christ Consciousness Spherical Breathing Technique

You begin by sitting in a comfortable, relaxed position. Close
your eyes and let the outside world go. When you feel calm
and relaxed, expand your feelings to a state of love and unity
for all life every where, and also visualize the star tetrahedron
around the body.

On the inhale of the first breath, visualize the male tetrahedron. This is the one with the apex facing up. The point at the
base of the tetrahedron, which is just above the knees when
you are standing, is facing toward the front for males and toward the back for females. Visualize to the best of your ability
this male tetrahedron filled with brilliant white light. Your body
is surrounded by this light.

*   Excerpted from *Nothing In This Book is True, but It's Exactly How Things Are* by Bob
       Frissell, © Frog, Ltd., 1456 Fourth St., Berkeley, California 94710, copyright 1994.

Also on this first breath arrange your hands, palms up, with the thumb and index finger lightly touching. This is a mudra. Do not allow any of your other fingers to touch one another.

Inhale through your nose in a deep, relaxed, rhythmic manner for approximately seven second, bringing the breath up from the stomach, then to the diaphragm, and finally to the chest. Do this all in one movement.

Then, without pausing at the top of the inhale, begin your exhale. Exhale slowly through your nose for approximately seven seconds. As you exhale, visualize the inverted female tetrahedron, the point at the level of the solar plexus facing the back for males and the front for females. Again visualize this tetrahedron filled with brilliant white light.

After you have completed the exhale in approximately seven seconds, relax and hold your breath for approximately five seconds. Move your eyes toward each other (look slightly cross-eyed, in other words), then look up and immediately look down to the ground as fast as you can. At the same time visualize the white light in the female tetrahedron shooting out through the apex of the tetrahedron and into the Earth.

As you are doing this, you should feel an electrical sensation moving down your spine. Drunvalo calls this pulsing. What you are doing is clearing out the negativity in the part of your electrical system that is associated with the mudra you used (index fingers and thumbs touching).

Immediately after pulsing the energy down your spine, begin the second breath. The second breath is exactly the same as the first breath except for a different mudra. For the second breath you hold the thumbs and second fingers together. Similarly, for breaths three through six, only the mudras differ.

For the third-breath mudra, hold the thumb and third finger (ring finger) together. For the fourth-breath mudra, hold the thumb and little finger together. For the fifth-breath mudra, hold the thumb and index finger together just as in the first breath. And for the sixth-breath mudra, hold the thumb and second finger together, just as in the second breath.

The next seven breaths begin a different breathing pattern. It is no longer necessary to visualize the male tetrahedron on the inhale and the inverted female tetrahedron on the exhale. Instead visualize the tube that runs through the body, extending one hand length above the head and one hand length below the feet. In other words, the tube runs through the apex of the male tetrahedron, which extends one hand length above the head. It also runs through the apex of the female tetrahedron, extending one hand length below your feet. The diameter of the tube is exactly the same as the diameter of the circle formed when your thumb and middle finger are touching.

Begin the seventh inhale immediately after the pulse following the sixth exhale. Inhale rhythmically, taking about seven seconds, just as you inhaled for the first six breaths. As you begin the seventh inhale, visualize the tube running through your body as well as brilliant white light running up and down the tube at the same time. In other words, visualize prana running down the tube from over your head and simultaneously running up the tube from beneath your feet.

The instant you begin the seventh inhale, brilliant white light runs up and down your tube. Now visualize the light meeting inside the tube at the level of the navel or third chakra. As the two beams of light or prana meet, a sphere of light or prana about the size of a grapefruit forms and slowly begins to grow.

As you continue to inhale for approximately seven seconds, the sphere of prana slowly grows. At the end of the seventh inhale, immediately begin your exhale. There is no more holding of the breath and no more pulsing.

For the next seven breaths use the same mudra, that is both the index and second fingers lightly touching the thumb with the palms up.

As you begin to exhale, the prana continues flowing from each end of the tube and expanding the sphere centered at the navel. By the time of the full exhale (approximately seven seconds), the sphere of prana will be about eight or nine inches in diameter.

Begin the eighth breath immediately after the seventh exhale. On the eighth breath the prana sphere continues to grow until it reaches its maximum size at the end of the exhale. At its maximum the sphere is roughly the size of a volleyball.

On the ninth breath, the sphere does not grow bigger, but gets brighter. Visualize the sphere growing brighter and brighter on both the inhale and exhale.

On the tenth breath, continue to visualize the sphere growing brighter. About halfway through the inhale, the sphere will reach critical mass and ignite into a sun. As you begin to exhale, make a small hole with your lips and force air out of your mouth. Then let it all go with a final whoosh. As you do, the ignited sun expands outward to form a sphere of charged white light or prana.

The sphere is not yet stable at this point, however. It took all your energy just to get it out there. It will take three more breaths to stabilize it.

The eleventh, twelfth and thirteenth breaths are needed to stabilize the sphere. Inhale and exhale just as you did for the seventh through ninth breath, all the while feeling the flow of prana through the tube, meeting at the navel, and expanding into the sphere around your body.

The sphere is now stabilized and you are ready for the all-important fourteenth breath. For the seventh through the thirteenth breaths, the prana flow met in the tube behind the navel. That tunes us to our third-dimensional reality. If we were going to stay here, we would stop after thirteen breaths. Since we are moving to the fourth dimension (I need to insert here that Drunvalo and many others believe we are moving physically into the fourth dimension which is different than just experiencing the fourth dimension through just the emotional, mental and spiritual bodies), the fourteenth breath becomes necessary in order to return us to that reality.

At the beginning of the inhale of the fourteenth breath, you move the point where the two streams of prana meet up from the navel to the sternum. The entire large sphere around your body moves up, as the original small sphere (still contained within the large sphere) rises to the sternum. Having the prana meet here tunes you to the fourth dimension or Christ consciousness.

As you do this, change the mudra. Males place the left palm on top of the right palm with the thumbs lightly touching; females place the right palm on top of the left palm with the thumbs lightly touching. Keep this mudra for the remainder of the meditation.

As you continue to breathe from your Christ-consciousness center, switch to shallow, relaxed breathing and let yourself feel the flow of prana and love for as long as you like. Drunvalo recommends spending at least ten minutes in this meditation.

It is very important to hold pure thoughts like love, truth, beauty, trust, harmony, and peace. The reason is that in the fourth dimension or Christ-consciousness, thoughts are instantly manifested into reality. (He is speaking of the tenth and higher levels of the fourth dimension, thoughts manifest instantly once you're PHYSICALLY in those levels of the fourth dimension, but until then, as you experience fourth dimensional reality through the emotional, mental and spiritual bodies, your thoughts will manifest at an accelerated rate with each level you move through in that dimension but not instantaneously).

As you continue to do this meditation, your awareness increasingly tunes to fourth-dimensional consciousness. As this is happening you also become increasingly aware of the power of your thoughts and how they are unerringly creating your reality. Your thoughts then begin to manifest into reality more and more quickly, hence the importance of holding absolutely pure thoughts.

If you choose to do this meditation, it is best to practice it daily until you have become a conscious breather, that is, remembering on every breath your intimate and inseparable connection to the One Spirit that moves through everything. It is only necessary to do the fourteen breaths once a day. From there you can remember to breathe through your tube and recreate your sphere at any time throughout the day.

This sphere of prana also forms a very powerful field of protection around you, second only to the merkaba. Your sense of safety and trust will increase as a result.

It is important in this meditation to visualize clearly the male tetrahedron on the inhale and female tetrahedron on the exhale of the first six breaths (this is true for both men and women), each filled with brilliant white light or prana.

I also find it helpful to trace the images of the tetrahedrons with my hands before I begin the meditation and while I am doing the first six breaths. In other words, I begin by tracing the male tetrahedron, first the base and then the sides, up to the point over my head. That seems to lock the image in place for me. I will also trace the base of the female tetrahedron at my solar plexus. I then visualize the point of the base behind my back and the sides going down until they form the apex in the ground.

It is necessary to know clearly your relationship to the star tetrahedron as you are standing or sitting. The apex of the male tetrahedron is always one hand length over your head, whether you are standing or sitting. Remember, if you are standing, the base of the male tetrahedron is just above your knees. If you sit down, the base moves down accordingly. That means, then, if you are sitting in a chair, the base is on the floor, or at least very close to that. If you are sitting on the ground, approximately one half of the male tetrahedron is in the ground.

The base of the inverted female tetrahedron is always at the solar plexus, whether you are standing or sitting. If you are standing, the apex of the female tetrahedron is one hand length into the ground. If you are sitting on the ground, more than one half of the female tetrahedron is in the ground.

As you continue to do this meditation, your ability to "see" the tetrahedrons, white light, tube and spheres will improve.

In order to take the next three breaths you must have permission from your higher self. Breaths fifteen through seventeen are the ones that set the counter-rotating fields of the merkaba in motion.

Summation

In summing up my own evolution, one realization stands out above all others: we are all beings of Light and we are growing at our own pace in our understanding of our own divinity. I do not need to compare myself or judge myself to anyone else. It is that simple.

We would do well to stay within our own experience and not use someone else's experience as the standard from which to go by. Each experience is unique to the individual experiencing it. Each life is different from every other life. We each hold a different piece of the divine plan. There are no duplicates.

May your journey be as joyfully rewarding and fulfilling as mine has been for me. Bless us, one and all.

PART 2

Additional Techniques and Information

I have compiled information on breathing and a couple more techniques that have assisted me and that may assist you. Hopefully, they may also satisfy your mental and emotional bodies. I have found that it is not the techniques that stay with you, but the truth behind them.

It has taken more than twenty years to get where I am today. This same journey can now be done in a much shorter period because every time a person achieves a realization, a path is formed, and then widens, so that it becomes easier for others to follow.

There is a technique in particular that I use but I don't know where I learned it. It has proven to be beneficial, especially when I'm stressed:

Imagine pushing outward (you can also use your physical hands if that makes your experience more real), at least a foot in all directions—top, bottom, front, sides, and back. Your attention is in your field of awareness in the present. Your intention is that you are expanding the energy envelope around you, making room for divine consciousness to enter, and opening yourself up to universal knowledge by allowing it to engulf your being.

You can use this technique first thing in the morning or any time during the day when you think of it. I like to use it when meditating, especially before multidimensional meditation or when my head feels like it has a tight band around it, which can happen when you're bringing in a lot of Light.

Breathing

It is important to know how to breathe consciously, so I present information from two sources. In the following excerpt from *Breathing** by Michael Sky, note how Michael relates attention and intention in terms of the breath:

> The primary and essential function of breath is reception and release. With each inhale, we open to, draw in, conduct, and thus receive the living, spiritual energies of the universe. With each exhale, we surrender, relax, radiate as love, and thus release all personal energies into universal relationship.
>
> Every such breath is a drink from God's own fountain and will provide the fundamental nourishment that humans require. Every such breath is a conscious movement of pleasure— throughout all levels of self—richly felt and deeply healing. And, truly, every such breath is deserved: we are children of breath, and the way is ever open for our return to a life divine and everlasting.
>
> With time, we may notice that our way of breathing perfectly reflects our way of life. The saying, "As we live and breathe..." is precisely true: we breathe to live, of course, and we live in the manner that we breathe.
>
> The inhale relates to will. It is the embodiment of INTENTION, drive, desire, wanting, and receiving. When there is a tired, negligible, or complacent inhale, it reflects similar attitudes toward life: "I can't, I don't want to, it's too much effort, it'll never work, I don't deserve it."
>
> When there is vital, urgent thirsting for each breath, it reflects a strong, inherent desire for life: the breather is inspired, and inspiring, and is gathering in the requisite energies of a creative life.
>
> Attention also must be given to the physical movement of each inhale. To live fully is to breathe in fully—to move and fill the whole torso with breath/energy. To breathe only into the upper chest is to avoid the strong, creative energies of the lower

---

*   Reprinted with permission from *Breathing*, by Michael Sky, Copyright 1990, Bear & Co., Santa Fe, NM.

abdomen and sexual organs. To breathe only into the belly is to avoid the equally strong, creative energies of the heart and throat.

Through observation of the inhale, we can see those areas of experience that the breather would avoid—areas where the breather's will is inhibited. Conversely, through consciously bringing the breath into such areas, the will is exercised and strengthened, and inhibiting patterns of contraction are finally resolved.

The exhale relates to surrender. It is the embodiment of letting go, relaxing, going with the flow, and releasing. The perfect exhale is completely effortless. It is, precisely, the cessation of all effort, of all doing, of all controlling. At the fullness of the inhale, all doing ceases; the breather surrenders, and the body exhales freely and completely.

Any effort added to the exhale effectively contracts the breather's energy. When, for instance, the breather holds the breath back, letting it out only slowly or not emptying out completely, the tension of that effort derives from and contributes to patterns of contraction. Such restrained and/or partial exhaling reflects a fundamental distrust toward life, perhaps a belief that there is not enough, and always a belief in the need to stay in control of events.

The breather might also add effort to the exhale by forcefully blowing the air out. Rather than releasing the breath, the breather is urgently pushing it away. Such exhaling reflects a belief that we are filled with "bad" energies, pains, thoughts, and feelings, and that if we work hard enough we can expel/purge them from our system.

It is important to remember that our patterns of contraction, and all possible manifestations of such patterns, are forever composed of energy—the energy of life itself. It is not the energy that is bad or unhealthy; rather, it is our choice to hold onto and contract it that is detrimental for us. That is, at some time in the past we were in the midst of a challenging event, with energy generating within us to meet the challenge, and we chose to contract. It is sustaining that choice now that hurts—not the "old" energy. And strenuously trying to rid oneself of "old" energy (trying to dump the garbage) only serves to add to contraction—is in fact a reflection of the original choice—while directly reinforcing the notion that the breather is inherently unhealthy. In the moment that we resolve such a choice, the long-contracted energy is released and experienced as joy. Indeed, resolving an old pattern is a gift of living, creative energy to the breather and to the surrounding environment.

To repeat, any effort added to the exhale effectively contracts the breather's energy, and actually derives from and adds to the breather's patterns of contractions. When we add effort to the exhale, we are creating hardship by working where no work is required and by struggling unnecessarily with a fundamentally free process of life.

Furthermore, as the exhale becomes stuck and inhibited, it becomes harder and harder to inhale fully. The less empty we become in breathing out, the less we can hope to fully breathe in anew. The more we hang onto the "stuff" of the past, the more we restrict our present and future potential. Indeed, most problems with an inhibited will/inhale actually begin as problems with surrendering/exhaling. Thus we should always pay close attention to the exhale and to any feelings and sensations of added effort.

Ultimately, a healthy, balanced, and creative life is composed of equal parts of will and surrender. We are the doer, exerting our personal will, and life is done magically through us the more we let go. We create the world and we surrender to its creations. We are going with the flow down life's river and we have the paddle of personal will to steer the way.

When there is too much personal will and not enough surrender or too much surrendering and a weak will, then life is unbalanced and creativity suffers. Such imbalance is always reflected in breath as an imbalance between inhalation/reception and exhalation/release. Conversely, by simply bringing consciousness to the breath—inhaling deeply and fully releasing the exhale—we can actively create resolution and balance, strengthening our personal will while greatly enhancing our capacity for surrender.

Still, as we have seen, we may struggle so with simply breathing—with simply receiving and simply releasing. Old patterns of contraction interfere and impede. Our lungs are filled with the dust of the past; we seem unable to get enough air, we urgently seem unable to really let go. To our great frustration, the more urgently we reach for more breath, the more we notice how little we breathe, and how often we stop breathing, and how easily we just forget the whole thing.

For whatever solace—and encouragement—it may provide, a growing awareness of how hard, and even painful, it is to breathe is actually a sign of progress. Prior to consciously working with the breath, most people have no awareness of their breathing at all, except when it seriously malfunctions. The conscious breather, in feeling and moving toward the full power and promise of the breath, becomes more acutely aware of tendencies to contract the breath that have always been unconsciously supported.

Conscious breathing obviously does not create contracted breathing—it reveals it. Thus, the conscious breather who is lately noticing breathing patterns—I never breathe when I talk to my mother, I didn't breathe through my entire commute to work, I seem to hold my breath whenever I think hard about something, I never breathe when I thank about money, I just can't get a full breath!—is actually breathing better than ever. The struggle is all a sign of healing, though certainly it is a measure of healing that goes down better with a steady patience and a good sense of humor.

Another aspect of the conscious breather's progress, with which we may also struggle, is a growing sense of vulnerability. Our patterns of contraction have long functioned as a form of protection, a literal suit of armor. That we no longer need the protection and that we are suffocating inside the armor does not seem to matter; we are accustomed to this way—it has worked for many years, and it feels safe.

To let go of our patterns of protection is to step out of the armor, naked and open to the world and all that it offers. This can be, to say the least, terrifying. However, we can only know how safe the world truly is, and how much love and support there is for each of us, by facing life without the armor. Our ideas about the world, formed from inside the armor, are always skewed, false, and limiting, though invariably self-confirming.

In approaching the world as vulnerable, we create a world that no longer threatens. This requires a leap of faith—many leaps of faith—and the courage to breathe in deeply in the midst of difficult times. When "I breathe it in and surrender!" has replaced "I contract from it" as our immediate response to stressful events, then we have transformed the world and our place within it.

Inhaling and exhaling, receiving and releasing, one continuous flow of life: without holding, without pushing, without contracting, and without effort...

Inhaling and exhaling, receiving and releasing, one continuous flow of life; with feeling, with pleasure, and with conscious attention to the ever-rising possibility of joy...

Simply breathing—simply choosing to breathe, now, with conscious, creative awareness—can be the resolution of all that has come before and the evolution of all to follow.

May your every breath bring you peace and joy.

May all beings breathe free and flourish.

And now to complete Michael's information on breathing, here is The Cleansing Breath Exercise:

Breathing in through the nose, with each inhale imagine, sense, feel, or believe that the air is coming in through the soles of your feet. Breathe in as if you have to pull the air up through your feet, ankles, legs, hips, and torso, until you blow it out through your open mouth. Continue for several breaths, drawing the air in through your feet and up through your body, and then blowing it out, slowly and calmly.

Now, continuing with this breath, imagine that as you draw the air up through your body you are sweeping along with it all of the contracted energy in your system. Breathe up through the feet, up through your body, sweeping along all contracted energies, and then blow them out-calmly, slowly, with the air. Feel this movement of air and the sweeping of energy as vividly as you can. Really feel it.

Now, imagine that as the swept-up energy hits the open air it bursts into a shower of sparks. Picture this, sense it, imagine that with every slow, calm exhale your swept-up energy bursts into a shower of bright sparks.

Continue for several minutes, observing all reactions and sensations.

Rebirthing

The second excerpt on the subject of breathing is by Bob Frissell, a practicing rebirther, and is excerpted from *Nothing in This Book Is True, but It's Exactly How Things Are.**

Rebirthing is a tool that enables you to directly experience the One Spirit that moves through everything. Not only that, rebirthing teaches in a way that allows you to create for yourself an inner experience of unity as an ongoing process.

The only way to unite with the Spirit is to discover it within. This is the only way, and in so doing you're uniting with the infinite power of the universe.

Rebirthing is much more than just breathing; it is a combination of consciously breathing energy along with correctly using your mind so that you bring the two into harmony, working in alignment with each other.

The practice we are talking about here is rhythmic breaths in which "inhale" and "exhale" are connected without any pause in between them. The emphasis is on the inhale; the exhale is totally relaxed. This type of breathing will facilitate the movement of energy in your body—very pure, very powerful light energy, the energy of the life force itself. The natural tendency of this energy is to bring to your attention anything that you are holding on to that is less pure than itself.

*   *Nothing in This Book Is True, But It's Exactly How Things Are* by Bob Frissell, ©Frog, Ltd., 1456 Fourth St., Berkeley, California 94710, copyright 1994.

Again, rebirthing is much more than just breathing. The process also includes expanding your ability to relax into, tune into, feel, and be at peace with whatever is going on in your body. This results in emotional resolution. The focus is on expanding to include all the physical sensations in your body, ranging from emotions to tingling, vibrating, and the like. These sensations will then gradually integrate into your greater sense of well-being. This enables you to let go of negativity you have been carrying around as a result of suppressing emotions.

Rebirthing is about completing the past. Incompletions from the past life in the body, in the form of what you might call stuck energy, are held in place by shallow breathing. (To those of you who have done any bodywork, it might be obvious what I am talking about here.)

Contrast rebirthing with the ways in which you might have dealt with unwanted emotions in the past. Let's take anger, for example. First, it is almost certainly not present-time anger, but most likely is an incompletion from the past being triggered by a present-time experience. this is how incompletions from the past work; they continue to manifest in present time and we usually resist. Around and around it goes. One way people deal with anger is to internalize it by denying it, suppressing it, or blaming oneself. Another way is to externalize it by blaming others, kicking and screaming, or acting it out in some other way. Neither way ever produces emotional resolution.

What works is to apply the process of rebirthing, that is, connected breathing, relaxing into the feeling, feeling it in exquisite detail, and continuing to make peace with what you are feeling.

Working at the feeling level is faster and much more direct than working directly with the mind. You do not need to have a cognitive understanding of what is happening. You can do it entirely at the level of sensation. That alone will change how your mind relates to the situation.

Fundamental to expanding your ability to relax into and feel bodily sensations is the context in which you are holding your experiences. At the very least you need to be willing for sensations to be the way they are, even if you don't like them.

This will work. Even more useful, however, is the willingness to hold everything you are feeling as a healing in process. By relaxing into and allowing your feelings on the deepest level you will create your own healing. Ultimately, this will lead you to a feeling of gratitude for things being just the way they are.

Keep in mind that the natural function of energy as it moves through your body is to bring to your attention whatever you have been suppressing or holding on to. That's just its physics, how it works. Thankfully, it does this a layer at a time—you do not get more than you can handle. A layer at a time, breath by breath, emotions or feelings that you have been avoiding are brought to your attention by the moving energy. "Avoiding" here implies that you have been judging that there is something about these emotions or feelings that is "wrong."

I want to lump a few terms together: make-wrong, judgment, and resistance. When I use one term I am generally connoting them all. So whenever you are judging something or making something wrong, what you are doing in effect is locking the energy in place. What is fundamentally important here is the willingness to change your mind about whatever it is you have been making wrong.

A rebirthing session operates in a setting of safety and trust, and this environment gives you an expanded ability to be with and relax into physical and emotional sensations and, in so doing, begin the process of their completion. Shifting to a positive context gives you an expanded ability to allow things to be the way they are, rather than resisting them. Whatever you and I resist not only persists but, in direct response to our resistance, also gets stronger. If we find a particular mood or sensation uncomfortable and avoid it, then its demands on us become stronger and harder to evade. We are giving it energy by resisting it. If you are breathing against resistance it is going to get magnified and multiplied. The very things you are avoiding almost magically confront you again and again at every turn. On the other hand, you can easily and effortlessly move through the same material and dissolve it by going with it.

When you are breathing energy and relaxing into and tuning into the sensations you are feeling in your body and allowing them to be the way they are, the healing process begins. This can be easy, pleasurable, and even blissful.

Now, having said all this, perhaps the most important point is that none of this has to be taken literally, none of it is chiseled in stone. The key factor, the most important aspect, is your willingness to participate in the process in the first place. Included here is the willingness to let go of whatever you have been holding on to and to feel that peace and happiness are more important for you than being right or getting even. This willingness is what allows everything else to happen. With this volition, you do not have to do anything else perfectly, and the session will be effective.

The most important factor, whether practicing how to ride a bike or learning to breathe energy, is your willingness to do it in the first place. That willingness alone gives you enormous freedom to just be. The freedom leads you to an expanded ability to relax and let energy flow.

In order to have a direct experience of the unity of being, you have to expand to include all of yourself. In other words, the habit of compartmentalizing yourself is a direct offshoot of duality, of creating your source externally as opposed to internally. The fragmentary parts of ourselves—incompletions from the past, things we are too fearful to be with—we tend to compartmentalize. We think we are putting them away, burying them so we won't have to deal with them. But this is fundamentally holding part of ourselves as shameful or wrong, and that part will always be exposed as less pure by the breath.

There is no possible way to experience unity of being when you are holding your life, your being, like this. Expanding your ability to accept the underlying safety and trust of the universe in the setting of a rebirthing session gives you an expanded ability to be with those things you have been resisting. As you experience them in this way, they begin literally to dissolve, and when they dissolve, your duality begins to dissolve also. That is, events arise and dissolve in breath. It matters little whether the events are childhood, birth, past life, or whatever you consider them to be. It matters only that there is stuck energy that is dissolving. What you are left with is the unity of being as a living presence within you. You have a direct—not a theoretical—experience of the living spirit in your body.

This is equivalent to saying there is integration of both sides of the brain. The conceptual male side fuses with the female intuitive side.

I emphasize that this is not a regressive process to take you back to birth, early childhood, and so on, even though memories of these experiences may come up for you in a session. What alone matters about these incompletions from the past is to discover what you are currently carrying with you in a way that continues to manifest in present time. Your best access to these feelings is in present time. What you are carrying with you in the form of stuck energy definitely feels like something, and you can access it in that way.

The process then is about breathing, relaxing, tuning into feelings, and shifting the way you have been habitually holding them in avoidance, resistance, and making wrong. The process is about expanding your identity breath-by-breath to include these feelings so that they can integrate into a greater sense of well-being. In doing so, the past begins to complete itself.

Learning to rebirth yourself from a professional rebirther gives you a tool that you can use anytime to spark emotional resolution and the experience of the unity of being.

Over time you will learn to rely more and more on your own authority rather than external authority. You will learn more and more how the Source is within, not without.

The teacher is the breath itself. It unfolds to you at its own rate. It moves at the rate that is perfect for you, which is never the same for any two people. Your breath is the vehicle to take you to your own Source, the higher self that resides within you.

The foundation of rebirthing is a simple exercise called Twenty Connected Breaths.

Twenty Connected Breaths

You can do this exercise throughout the day, whenever you feel the need. However, it is recommended that for the first week you only do it once daily:

1. Take four short breaths.

2. Then take one long breath.

3. Pull the breaths in and out through your nose.

4. Do four sets of the five breaths, that is, four sets of four short breaths followed by one long breath without stopping, for a total of twenty breaths.

Merge the inhale with the exhale so the breath is connected without any pauses. One inhale connected to one exhale equals one breath. All twenty breaths are connected in this manner so you have one series of twenty connected breaths with no pauses.

Consciously pull the inhale in a relaxed manner and let go completely on the exhale while continuing to keep the inhale and exhale the same length.

Use the long breath to fill your lungs as completely as you comfortably can on the inhale, and to let go completely on the exhale.

Breathe at a speed that feels natural to you. It is important that the breathing be free and natural and rhythmical, rather than forced or controlled. This is what enables you to breathe prana as well as air.

Since most of us have developed bad breathing habits you might experience some physical sensations, such as light headedness or tingling sensations in your hands or elsewhere. If you do this exercise daily, you will notice that the sensations may change and become less overwhelming, and more generative of healing. This indicates that you are learning about breathing consciously and are getting direct benefits in your body.

Daily practice of this exercise will teach you more about breathing than you have ever learned in your entire life.

If you wish to accelerate the process, contact a professional rebirther.

It's About Time

Here is a technique from a tape called *It's About Time** by Jann Weiss. I have found it to be a very important addition to my repertoire for solving issues. Like myself, I am sure you can find numerous applications for this technique.

Lately the word "time" is being redefined. It is no longer being perceived as linear but as something that is all present, all now. Imagine for instance, sitting with twenty people around a very large table, each with a bowl of some kind of food. Everyone takes from the bowl in front of them, passes it to the right, and then takes from the next bowl as it's handed to them. In this way, it is just a matter of time before each gets to the twentieth dish. But let's say there are sweet potatoes across the table from you. You really want butter melted on those sweet potatoes and if you wait until they get around to you, they'll be too cold. You have the ability to reach across the table, snag that bowl of sweet potatoes, grab one out of the bowl and put butter on it "now." We don't have to wait until it is "time." It is possible to reach anywhere in time and obtain what we need. And this is what this session is about.

With the use of Level I within this process, we've already been working in our past. We've been going into our childhood, into past lives, even back to the beginning of Creation. Our past has been very easy for us to access.

Here is a technique for taking a future self and presenting what it knows to your body "now." Let's imagine for a moment that you have an addiction that you've been fighting for several years. You despair of ever healing this addiction; you feel you should be able to do but you just don't seem to be succeeding. This technique taps into the part of you that is beyond the addiction, to the future you where you've healed the addiction. You can tap into that future self and that future time. You can open up and allow in what that future self knows.

---

*   *It's About Time*, The Living in Truth Institute, 1994.

The first thing your body will learn, is that it *is* healable. The addiction is obviously healable—it has been done in your future. That is incredibly empowering for your body when it's holding an "I can't" belief. Or if it believes that "I'll die if I do," then the future self is proof that you are not going to die. Presenting the body with new data is a short cut to actually bringing the body around to allowing the healing.

Many of us are impatient in our healing, and might, say, try to squeeze five lifetimes worth of healing in this one life. Now that's awfully quick. But now we've gotten to a point where we feel that taking an entire lifetime is still too long. Then we're going to get to a point where five years is too long. Then we're going to want it in a couple of months, a couple of weeks. The technique of tapping into the future self can do this for us, quickening it in a way that the body can handle. You must not go faster than the body can handle or you will overwhelm it and it will take you out of the race entirely. It just won't let you work. So we are trying to find ways to go faster, which is what our minds want, without overwhelming the body. This is one of the ways.

Also, the entire universe is shifting in such a manner that will systematically eliminate all negativity, and we are at a point in time where we are conscious enough to catch it happening and be part of it. Our future selves affect us not to make a difference in their time, but also in ours.

Of course, the universe has always been evolving, but something else is also going on. As a species, we are becoming aware of this whole operation and can incorporate it into our own shift. We can use the cosmic shift to speed up our own.

In a meditation I was shown an inverted pyramid. It represented my work. The base, or the point of the pyramid was the Level I process mentioned earlier. It was designed for working on a cellular level, to start the shift in the body, to start the reprogramming in the body. The top (or wide part of the pyramid) represented the multi-dimensional work that we were beginning.

Through the process in Level I, we are able to phase in and use the realities from higher dimensions. What we found, however, was that the body resisted letting those realities in. We could get only so far and the body said, "No more, this is just too strange; I can't integrate it, can't live it, can't do it." So, I've created a middle section on the pyramid—the use of Time. Once we get comfortable with redefining the reality of time, then it will be easier for us to allow more of the multi-dimensional information in.

Understand, our body is afraid that if we open to the higher dimensions or what I call etheric realities, then we will become etheric and cease to exist. As far as your body is concerned, that is death.

We are trying to show the body that if you integrate these realities, you enhance the body, not terminate it. If you open to the future and allow future self to influence you, you will heal faster. Using "time" for healing is a way of stretching the physical body beyond its boundaries and its sense of itself.

Process # 1

Take a deep breath...straighten your spine...uncross your limbs...relax

Close your eyes, go inside...just be with your body for a moment...notice how your body feels.

Allow yourself to open to your own higher soul self, the part of you that is all knowing...that is ancient...that has your plan...the part of you that animates you

Breath your soul self in...give it permission to interact with your physical form

Now allow yourself to look into your past and find one pivotal point in your past...one time when something important was going on in your life

Let it come to mind...take the first one that comes to your mind

How old were you?...say your age out loud

Take a look at the "you" then...what is that you're doing?

Find a time when that "you" was asleep...see yourself at that age asleep

Focus on your body here and now and breath your Soul's I Am-ness in

Now focus that I Am-ness back to the sleeping "you"...how that sleeping body lets the I Am-ness in

Continue breathing the I Am-ness into your body now and feel it give to the sleeping "you" back then

See how the sleeping "you" absorbs the energy and integrates everything that it needs...see how it absorbs your Soul's I Am-ness into the places where it's afraid.

Focus the soul's energy into any fear or self-doubt that that sleeping body may be holding

Just keep breathing the I Am-ness in, flowing it back and focusing it into any fear or darkness that the sleeping body is holding...take your time here

See how the past "you" is being filled with the I Am-ness... can you feel the love?

Some of you will notice as you do this that you are beginning to feel a love for that past "you"

Don't try to make it happen...just notice and keep breathing... keep allowing the flow to the sleeping self

continue directing the flow to any fear the sleeping body may be holding

See truth in that body...what is that body's truth?

Can you feel the soul in that sleeping body?

Focus on what you know spiritually in you "now" body

Focus on where your spiritual evolution has brought you

Direct this information back to your sleeping self...allow the sleeping self to be filled with what you know...about how multi-dimensional you are...about how you are God expressing itself...about how supported you are...how loved you are

Allow the transfer of this information from your "now" body to your "then" body...letting it takes it fill...putting the information everywhere it needs it

Look to see what is happening to that body as it takes the information in

Now as you're watching that body sleeping there, look in the room and see who else is in the room around the body... can you see the angel?

Can you see the aspect of soul?...all supporting that sleeping "you"

Help the sleeping body to be aware of the support that is around

You are back in time, supporting "you" back then

You are one of your own guides in your past

Now allow yourself to again become aware of the future "you" behind you...focusing through your "now" body... focusing everything it knows about you...feed your truth to you

How loved you are, how supported you are

Let that information in...let it fill you...and see how your future "you" feels the same way about you as you feel about the past "you"

Now, allow your future self to continue focusing this information through your body to the body of the past sleeping "you"

Allow the sleeping body to be filled with self-love and self-acceptance

Let the dreams be filled with it...allow the healing

Allow the flow from behind...self-love through you...flowing into the past you...asleep on the bed...filling with self-love

Breathe in the words, "I AM"

Feel all three of you co-existing...I am this...these three points in Time..."I AM"

Breathe it in

Release your awareness from your past self...gently leaving it to continue in the dream state

Thank your future "you" for working with you...release it and bring your awareness back to your body now

Take a deep breath...say out loud, "I AM"...and your first name...again, out loud, "I AM"...and your first name.

Now come on back into the room.

Do not worry if you cannot form a real concept of your future self. You may not at first. It will just be a hint of something behind you. It may not be clearly delineated. You'll have more of a sense of what is being projected to you in terms of how your future self comprehends you. It is as if you are in very cloudy water with dolphins. You can't see the dolphins but you have a definite sense of their presence, of what mood they are in, and whether they are actually focused on you or just passing by.

As you do this process, you may notice that the future self was behind you and the past self was in front of you. That is really interesting, because we normally think of the future as ahead and the past as behind.

After using this technique, someone commented, "When I was focusing back to the past existence I could feel the compassion, but when the future self was behind me, I felt more of a bond. The compassionate feeling was heightened incredibly."

Someone else said, "As soon as I try to get any kind of focus on the future, I feel I have no clue what my future is, even tomorrow." Avoid looking for details and information. Look for a you in the future, not what you are doing. You exist in the future as a living you, a "you" that is in form, having an experience, right now, only then. So deal with that future self in the same way you'd ask your higher soul self or angel to come and support you. Ask your future self to come and support you.

Also, trust your instincts (your soul) about the point in time you need to go back to. You may not necessarily know why the time you found yourself in was a pivotal point."

In the next process, we to back to the same time and this time we will allow in more of the future.

Process # 2

Take a deep breath...straighten your spine...uncross your limbs...relax

Close your eyes, go inside...just be with your body for a moment...notice how your body feels

Always take a moment to be with your body

Open to your higher soul self...give it permission to support you in what you are about to do

Focus again on the "you" in the past...see that person sleeping on the bed

You can look into that person and see any fear...that person is you

See how that past self feels about him or herself

Feel for any self-judgment...does that past "you" feel confident or intimated?

What is the biggest fear in that body?

Breathe your I Am-ness into that sleeping body

Focus that I Am-ness right into that fear...and breathe the words "we are the I AM" right into that fear...take your time

Keep breathing the words "we are the I AM" into that fear...we are the I AM...we can feel this, you and I

Feel to that sleeping self how the *two* of you are working on that fear

Just keep allowing your I Am-ness and the Truth of your I Am-ness to flow into the fear

Take your time...allow the healing in your past self

Feel the changes happening in that body

Now be aware that your future self is standing again behind you...focusing into you everything it knows

Allow its expanded sense of I Am-ness and self-acceptance to also flow into the fear

Feel how you and the future "you" are making a difference in the past "you"

Let yourself feel the healing that is going on there...what a dream your past self is having

Continue allowing the future self to work through you, affecting the past "you"

Allow it to happen through your body

What else does your past self need to know?...allow the future self to project that through you

Allow your future to talk to your past through you...through the dreams...allow the healing

Do you see how much information the sleeping "you" is taking in?

It's as though that future "you" is reaching right through you and touching the sleeping past self...let them talk

What else does the sleeping "you" need to know? What else?

The body is asking for a lot right now so we're going to take the time

Just keep allowing the future self to reach through and touch the fear being held in that body

Look how deep the energy is going...see how the soul is working to direct the future self's energy to where it needs to go

You may notice, the soul directing the energy into past lives

Just let it go through the sleeping form...don't try to see too much or do anything about it

Continue to allow the future self reaching through you, to that sleeping body

Take a deep breath...feel the future "you" behind you, holding you in your truth...holding you in such absolute love

Feel yourself holding that sleeping form in the past with absolute acceptance

Feel the "I AM" flowing through all three of you

Feel the oneness of all three of you...breathe in "I AM this"..."I AM"...Breathe it in

Now gently release yourself from the past "you" leaving it to complete in the dream state and come back now

Thank your future self and release it

Say out loud "I AM"...and your first name

Again, "I AM"...and your first name

Come back in the room.

This process works because we allow a future self to access a past self in a way using the "now self" as a buffer. In taking your more healed "now you" back, you present a more healed you to a less healed "past you." That starts the healing process so the "past you" can more easily accept the information and perspective of your "future you." It is important to keep holding your "now self" as a buffer.

Also, don't try to facilitate your past self during this process. Just allow the future self to flow through you to the past self. They will decide in the past self's dream state how much or how little to do. You just keep the focus on the future flowing through you to the sleeping body.

One of the ramifications of working on the past self is you're affecting you *now*. As you allow the future to flow through, you, a ripple shifts the whole time-line. The concentration may be a little difficult sometimes because of this.

Get out of the way and allow the healing, allow the flow until it feels complete. You'll know when it is complete. And when you leave the past self sleeping like that, he or she will finish what is needed.

In the next process, we go back again, but to a different time.

Process # 3

Take a deep breath...close your eyes...go inside and be with your body

Take the time to be with your body

Notice how your body feels

Open to your higher soul self, give it permission to support you in this work

Now allow yourself to open to a "you" that is five thousand years in the future

Don't look...don't try to see...just *feel* the presence of that future "you"

What does that future "you" feel like?

Now ask that future self to position itself behind you. Feel for the you that existed five thousand years ago

Don't look for the time...*feel* for "you" five thousand years ago

Allow yourself to feel what the past "you" feels like

Begin to allow the future self behind to flow through you and touch the "you" of five thousand years ago.

Allow that touch to flow through

Come slowly back to your body "now," continuing to be aware of the future self behind you and release that five thousand year old you...release it to its truth

Know that what you've just done has somehow changed it

Don't look to see what the change is...just give yourself permission to know that it's actually happening

Now be aware of your "now self"

Feel the future "you" working with the now "you"

The future "you" is beginning to merge with your body... allow it

Take your time

On a cellular level, this future aspect is communicating with your body

You are becoming one with your future self...and more specifically, with what your future self knows about you

Breathe it in...let it go anywhere in your body that it needs to go

What is the Truth about you?...what is the one thing you have in common with your future self?

What is the part of you that remains, that still exists five thousand years from now?

Allow the information into your body

A lot of information is being communicated to your body right now Your truth...you are the I AM

Feel the connection between you and your future self

Feel how mutual your healing is to both of you...how important it is to both of you and how accessible that future self is

You can call on this future self anytime, indeed, all the time

You can align with it...bring it into your body and give it the freedom to express itself through you...to communicate to you...to support you in integrating a new perspective

Allow yourself to feel the love

How much love does your future self feel for you?...a genuine appreciation and enthusiasm for your existence bordering on joy

It is pleased with you...look at what you're doing

As your future self supports you in this, it is changing its level of evolution as well

It is getting something out of this too but don't try to figure out what

Just be aware that it benefits from supporting you

Remember, all time is available to us now

The entire universe is shifting because of what we are doing... and what we are doing is because the entire universe is shifting

Notice how your body feels...be with your body

Thank your future self...release it back to its time

Take a deep breath...say out loud, "I AM"...and your first name

Say it again...and again

Come back into the room.

Sometime in the next three days, you will feel the urge to do this again. Then again soon after that you will be asked to do it again. Each time you repeat this process that the experience becomes deeper.

Another use for this process is to resolve an issue that is bothering you:

1. Align with the future self

2. Focus on the issue, taking the time to focus on how you *feel* about it.

3. Open to how your future self feels about it

This discharges the negative energy of the issue and provides a new perspective on it. It is the Level I process using a future self. You may find, after doing this process, that the issue is just not as important or you may have a very clear sense that it's handled somewhere in the future.

Your life may change dramatically if you let yourself use these processes. They are short cuts for your healing. Have fun with them.

Thank you for this opportunity to be of service...and Be in Peace.

Reality

Reality is based in the mind; it is perceptual. Within the mind is located the intersection of all that is "outside" and all that is "inside." That means the mind connects with the mental, emotional, spiritual, and the physical bodies and receives any and all input that is perceived as coming from the outside or from the inside of its physical vehicle.

The mind is beyond the thoughts and patterns of the brain. It is an organizing power. After the mind has taken in all available information, it organizes the input, and then interacts with the consciousness.

The consciousness extends beyond time and space. It is a total composite of you as a person, an accumulation of all that you have ever tasted, smelled, heard, felt and seen, including your responses to those stimuli. The consciousness is an aspect of the soul. Once the mind interprets newly organized information from all the input and combines it with the response of the consciousness, the mind then puts forth its perception of reality. It does this by releasing a pattern of thought-form energy through the energy fields of the physical body.

The universe is an ever-changing, always evolving energy field that processes trillions of levels of intelligence. It picks up the pattern of thought-form energy being given off through the energy fields of the physical body and rearranges itself around them. These thought-forms are electromagnetic in nature so any energy out in the universe that resonates with them will be attracted to the energy the mind is emitting.

Physical, emotional and mental actions are expressions of the qualities in the thought-forms that your mind transmits as its reality. If something comes into your reality and does not resonate with your present thought-form energy pattern, it will leave. Thus the reality you experience is created by energy, events, people, and situations that are attracted to you because of the thought-forms you transmit constantly out into the universe. Hence the popular sayings, "You create your own reality," and , "The universe rearranges itself to accommodate your picture of reality."

Before we look at how you can change your picture of reality, and hence your reality, one point must be clarified. You might say something like, "Well, if the universe arranges itself to accommodate my mind's idea of reality, which is being held in these thought-forms, and this reality includes my relationships and environment, then you are trying to tell me that I *like* having an abusive relationship and living in a dump!" Again, what I am saying is that, based on your patterns, which have an electromagnetic charge, you will attract what is in alignment with them and repel what is not. How that specifically manifests in your reality has to do with what is available around you.

Let me try to explain this in another way. Let's say it is time once again for the spirit that is you to come into a physical body. Your soul, the natural consciousness of life, resides just above the physical body because the environment of the physical body needs to be prepared before the soul can fully reside in it. So the soul uses an aspect of itself—the consciousness—to be in constant interaction with the mind.

The most important information the soul holds is the knowledge and experience of being one with everything. The purpose of its interaction with the mind is to allow the soul to express itself.

The consciousness is endowed with intelligence and it is energized by emotion. It is a forever-changing energy that can be influenced by the mind as easily as it can influence the mind.

The consciousness has within it all the thought-forms that have been accumulated throughout the lifetimes you have already experienced, for the soul and the consciousness never die. The consciousness just stores information in the form of these thought-forms and expands itself by adding more thought-forms to its energy field. The consciousness and the mind are interacting constantly. First the mind organized the input it has received, then it interacts with consciousness.

Finally, you are ready to be born, to come into body. As soon as your spirit moves into the body, you lose conscious awareness of being one with everything; the memory of oneness is veiled. From that first moment of entry into the body, everything you encounter that is other-than-you is taken in. This input enters through many channels; the channels you are the most familiar with are the senses, but input also enters through the spiritual, mental and emotional bodies as well as from the brain, organs and glands.

The mind then starts its sorting and organizing process. Then the mind interacts with the consciousness. Once that interaction is complete, the mind comes to its final interpretation. This final interpretation is then sent back out through all of the channels of input in the form of patterned electromagnetic thought-forms. So the whole body and its energy field are giving off these thought-forms orchestrated by the mind. The universe rearranges around them, helping to create the reality the mind is projecting. This is done through the electromagnetic field which attracts or repels whatever is needed to create the reality your mind has interpreted as being real for you.

The flow is constant, whether it be input coming in or the interpretation going out. The mind can transform its interpretation only by receiving new input. The consciousness interacts because the soul wants to reside in the physical body but knows it cannot be invited in until all energy bodies are balanced and sufficiently aligned with the physical body.

It is incredible how fast the mind can take in information, sort it, organize it, interact with other energy before coming to an interpretation, and then radiate that interpretation out into the universe so that the universe can rearrange itself around your picture of reality. The universe then reflects back to you in the form of experiences, events, and situations.

Because of the veiling at birth of your awareness of being one with everything, the mind's interpretation of the input it receives through an infant or a child often becomes distorted. This distortion is created because we are placed in a react-or-respond mode to circumstances in our environment as though we are separate from our environment. Since the mind cannot relate to the oneness, when it sorts the input and interacts with the consciousness, the interaction is taking place with thought-forms that have already been misinterpreted. This mis-interpretation is, of course, reinforced by the environment so it then becomes the foundation for your physical, emotional and mental responses, until you recognize yourself as independent of circumstances.

As you develop, input increases through exposure to new ideas and information, thus expanding the field of awareness around you, which includes the energy bodies, mind and consciousness. In considering new input, however, you sometimes experience blocks—dense energy held in the physical body that must be released and/or transformed. Fear holds this dense energy in place. But fear is merely an interference pattern, and may simply be fear of the pain attached to the content of the dense energy.

In any case, remaining open to new input in a particular area might mean dealing first with blocked energy in that area. That is what is referred to as "getting beyond your limitations," because the energy block limits your expansion.

For example. let's say you are the parent of a teenager who has asked for the use of your car. You know that this child is responsible, that he got an A in driver's training, that you have taught him the value of things, and that he has never disappointed you in matters of importance. But there is something inside you that just can't let go and let him use the car. It is so disturbing to you that you can actually feel your body tense up in some way.

Then an incident from your childhood flashes into your thoughts. You remember being yelled at and being made to feel irresponsible and a failure because of an experience with your parents' car. You are now feeling the pain of that long-ago incident and you realize that you have been holding not only that pain, but in addition, a multitude of responses around that pain that range from wanting to control your child to the fear of how you will respond if the same scenario occurs with your child. The fear of the pain holds you.

Then you realize why it has been so important to you to teach your child to be responsible, and you know you have done a good job. You are now able to release the fear and make your decision, for you have the confidence that if something should go wrong, you will deal with it more appropriately than your parents did.

All the input you have experienced has allowed the fear holding the block in place to be released, and the energy block is in the process of being transformed. It is not the experience of loss that is most important, but how the experience is registered in the body. The result is that you feel relief in the area of the body where the energy block was present.

It is important to identify the event that encouraged the blocked energy to make itself known. In this example it was the request for the car. Identifying the trigger will help you to find whatever additional input is needed. That new input will expand your mind and consciousness, creating a change in interpretation, so that new thought-forms will result in the release and transformation of the energy block. In this process, you embrace your humanness, and as a result of going beyond your energy blocks, you will expand your consciousness.

This expansion of consciousness is referred to as a consciousness shift. Through a series of consciousness shifts, enlightenment is attained. You attain enlightenment through the full participation of your entire being. The consciousness is evolving—it never stops expanding—but to help it along toward a shift, you need to open certain spaces within yourself. This means transforming limiting perceptions or energies and being in an open, allowing state so you can receive new input and new energy. Through enlightenment comes descension, the embodying of a vaster part of yourself. Descension occurs when you create enough space to receive a consciousness shift, and there is no limit to the number of times that this can happen. Descension is what I experienced as a result of the triggering effect of reading *Hind's Feet on High Places.*

Gradually, ascension happens organically after the process of descension. Eventually, the body is carrying so much Light that it physically shifts dimensions. In the process of ascension, the body mutates from being carbon-based to being Light-based.

The initiations that allow evolution by expanding consciousness so more Light can be received are nothing but the soul's experience of higher vibrational levels. With each point of realization that is integrated, the mind's reality reconstructs itself. Since everything in the universe vibrates and every stratum has its own agenda, evolution is nothing more than assimilating the experiences on each stratum, overcoming them, and then achieving a higher level of consciousness through that integration. Again, all is in the mind, and the more you can increase the frequencies of the thought-forms you hold, the closer to oneness you can be. And because you constantly transmit your thought-forms, the more you affect the thought-forms held by those around you.

The initiations give you opportunities to bring Light from the Source into your body. An initiation is the activation and eventual integration of the Source's Light located on that particular stratum of the physical body. These initiations, or points, are the levels of self that exist on all levels, from the physical body to the Source. As you move through these initiations, a clarification of your vibrations takes place. If for some reason you are unable to continue (for example, if fear comes up and blocks your energy), your soul will set up a more appropriate time for you to pass through that initiation. As you proceed through the initiations, you realize that you have already existed at each of those points. That is the realization of your identity as spirit, of your oneness with the Source.

A few people have written about the initiations from their understanding, limited as it might have been by the time at which they were on the planet and the filtering of their personalities. Alice Bailey wrote of them in the 1920s and 1930s. Brian Grattan in *Mahatma I & II*, also wrote in detail of initiations. Brian's perspective was that 352 levels exist and that during your time here on the planet, you could embody only 12 initiations before you had to leave the physical body because it could not hold any more Light. While Brian may be limited in his perception, it is through the efforts of people like him, as they explore and leave a trail to follow, that others learn to raise their vibrations.

There seems to be a strong focus on the initiation process—the numbering of it and the identifying of each one—so I will discuss my perception of it. The initiatory process is looked at as a measure of achievement. It *can* be a diversion that keeps you involved with attempting to fix yourself and prevents you from following your spirit. It can also keep you from co-creating Heaven on Earth because you are paying so much attention to what level you're on. Playing into the ego with "who's more highly initiated than who" allows for enormous amounts of spiritual ambition and pride.

Focusing on what you don't have causes the universe to rearrange around that, giving you more and more of the same. When you focus on the specifics of initiations, they can become infinite, and you will create more of them to achieve.

It really doesn't matter how many levels there are between the physical self and the Self already in existence at the Source level. The purpose is to come to self-realization at each point, whereby you embody all of who you are from here, to and including the Source. By making that your intention, you will avoid being side-tracked by the energies of comparing, judging, and earning. The time has come, instead of identifying and numbering the pathway, to just be with it.

There is a very deep level of energy in the human structure that is afraid of being complete with something. The numbering and identification of the initiations feed into that. It is a top-down, "you're-the-master-I'm-not" kind of energy.

Instead, we would benefit greatly now from a focus that said, "We are already perfect, we are divine beings, we are all multidimensional masters." I have taken to describing the initiation process as integrating a point or points of realization through Light and not identifying which one in particular an individual is experiencing.

As the mind and consciousness expand, the field of awareness (present reality) expands, creating a broader range of choices to respond to physically, emotionally, and mentally. How do we direct the mind's choices? We already know that in order to change the interpretation by the mind we need new input. Of course, Light itself is also new input, for it can teach and heal. This is true, but there's more: in order to end up with a specific interpretation as the result of all the new input into the mind, you need to direct the energies of the transformation in a specific direction. You do this by designing an intention for a desired result. In other words, the process of creating is generated by the creation itself. That is why your intention is so important—it is the reaching beyond yourself to bring something into being.

The intention is the trigger that allows the interpretation to move in a specific direction. The intention is an active participant in the process of transformation. It has this power because it takes responsibility. Using intention is a way of being the creator of what you want in the "future." Taking this step in responsibility for yourself and the directing of your reality is the beginning of the co-creator process, because it is important not to use intention carelessly and unconsciously.

Now let us talk about how you can use it to co-create your reality in a conscious way. The steps for conscious use are simple.

The Use of Intention

The first step is *attention*. Through attention, a desired situation comes to your awareness, and you design an *intention* for change.

It is important to avoid feeling an attachment to the outcome of an intention, for the stronger your attachment to an intention is, the less you are functioning in the present, and that throws the lower bodies out of balance. Another reason for not being strongly attached is so that any adjustments can be made that are necessary for manifestation.

The mind picks up on the intention and with its organizing abilities connects to the intention any input (resources) that is in alignment with that intention. The attention carries focus in its energy and the intention carries desire in its energy; so the mental body connects with the attention and the emotional body connects with the intention, merging together and working for a result. What about the spiritual body and the physical body? We know all of this takes place within the physical body, but what is not as apparent is how the spiritual body contributes.

The spiritual body taps into the divine plan, which contains all possible outcomes. It therefore encompasses all of the potential you are not yet able to use. It is a ladder you may climb, but you do so by interacting with the emotional, mental and physical bodies. In other words, you utilize your other bodies to climb the ladder of awareness, the unlimited potential of the divine plan.

The physical part of the journey is a very purposeful thrust into a greater understanding of who and what you are. The vibrational pattern of physical existence itself moves on the creative process. Life in physical existence shows you how you are doing in creating your own life and mirrors what you have created. It is the nature of physical existence that creates this mirroring effect, which can reflect who you are in the moment, what you hold to be true, what you are judging, and what you fear. The physical vibration shows you what you are bringing forth through your creative process, and whether or not you have accepted any limitations or restrictions.

The emotional body can be used to propel you beyond the cycling syndrome often found around limitation or restriction. The emotional body can also support the physical and mental bodies by moving energy, assisting the climb toward your spiritual potential.

The mental body is absolutely essential for its processing, but it must be integrated with the other aspects in order for you to be able to use it to climb the ladder of awareness. So the mental body plays a vital part in the discovery process, but you must remember that it has a limited perspective.

The Unified Chakra

Most people's physical, emotional, mental, and spiritual bodies are not merged. There are ways of accomplishing that union and I recommend one in particular. It is called the *Invocation to the Unified Chakra* and can be found in *What is Lightbody?** by Archangel Ariel channeled through Tashira Tachi-ren.

This invocation teaches the lower bodies to merge, then unify, so the oversouls (see the glossary) can hook in through them and live in the physical body. It also creates a force field around the body, allows you to handle vaster and vaster energies without your body becoming overwhelmed, and helps you to live completely in the now.

---

* *What Is Lightbody?* ©1995 by Tashira Tachi-ren, Oughten House Publications, Livermore, CA. Reproduced by permission

Invocation to the Unified Chakra

I breathe in Light
Through the center of my heart,
Opening my heart
Into a beautiful ball of Light,
Allowing myself to expand.
I breathe in Light
Through the center of my heart,
Allowing the Light to expand,
Encompassing my throat chakra
And my solar plexus chakra
In one unified field of Light
Within, through, and around my body.

I breathe in Light
Through the center of my heart,
Allowing the Light to expand,
Encompassing my brow chakra
And my navel chakra
In one unified field of Light
Within, through, and around my body.

I breathe in Light
Through the center of my heart,
Allowing the Light to expand,
Encompassing my crown chakra
And my base chakra
In one unified field of Light
Within, through, and around my body.

I breathe in Light
Through the center of my heart,
Allowing the Light to expand,
Encompassing my Alpha chakra
(Eight inches above my head)
And my Omega chakra
(Eight inches below my spine)
In one unified field of Light
Within, through, and around my body.
I allow the Wave of Metatron
To move between these two points.
I AM a unity of Light.

I breathe in Light
Through the center of my heart,
Allowing the Light to expand,
Encompassing my eighth chakra
(Above my head)
And my upper thighs
In one unified field of Light
Within, through, and around my body.
I allow my emotional body to merge
With my physical body.
I AM a unity of Light.

I breathe in Light
Through the center of my heart,
Allowing the Light to expand,
Encompassing my ninth chakra
(Above my head)
And my lower thighs
In one unified field of Light
Within, through, and around my body.
I allow my mental body to merge
With my physical body.
I AM a unity of Light.

I breathe in Light
Through the center of my heart,
Allowing the Light to expand,
Encompassing my tenth chakra
(Above my head)
And to my knees
In one unified field of Light
Within, through, and around my body.
I allow my spiritual body to merge
With my physical body,
Forming the unified field.
I AM a unity of Light.

I breathe in Light
Through the center of my heart,
Allowing the Light to expand,
Encompassing my eleventh chakra
(Above my head)
And my upper calves
In one unified field of Light
Within, through, and around my body.
I allow the Oversoul to merge
With the unified field.
I AM a unity of Light.

I breathe in Light
Through the center of my heart,
Allowing the Light to expand,
Encompassing my twelfth chakra
(Above my head)
And my lower calves
In one unified field of Light
Within, through, and around my body.
I allow the Christ Oversoul to merge
With the unified field.
I AM a unity of Light.

I breathe in Light
Through the center of my heart,
Allowing the light to expand,
Encompassing my thirteenth chakra
(Above my head)
And my feet
In one unified field of Light
Within, through, and around my body.
I allow the I AM Oversoul to merge
With the unified field.
I AM a unity of light.

I breathe in Light
Through the center of my heart,
Allowing the Light to expand,
Encompassing my fourteenth chakra
(Above my head)
And to below my feet
In one unified field of Light
Within, through, and around my body.
I allow the Source's Presence to move
Throughout the unified field.
I AM a unity of Light.

I breathe in Light
Through the center of my heart.
I ask that
The highest level of my Spirit
Radiate forth
From the center of my heart,
Filling this unified field completely.
I radiate forth throughout this day.
I AM a unity of Spirit.

After the Invocation to the Unified Chakra has trained the four bodies to merge, the chakras will change from disk-like shapes into spherical vortices. This allows your entire system to be attuned to the heart chakra. As the emotional, mental, and spiritual bodies merge and begin to build a co-creative relationship with the physical, the oversoul, the Christ Oversoul and the I AM Presence/I AM Oversoul can begin to hook through into the physical. Many times people access the Christ Oversoul but do not integrate it into the lower bodies or they access the oversouls before the lower bodies have unified and built a co-creative relationship with the physical. That means there is nothing for the oversouls to hook into.

Unification is essential for the oversouls to be able to occupy the physical body. Absence of such unification can lead to emotional instability or mental or physical illness. I have seen it manifest as a mild upset, flu-like symptoms, depression, a short-term loss of appetite—it all depends upon the individual. I mention these symptoms just to emphasize the importance of discernment and responsibility in your process of evolution.

The Source

A possible view of the Source might be helpful in understanding the idea of being one with everything.

Let us contemplate the entity I call the Source: It just exists in pure timelessness. The energy of Source radiates unconditional love and contains all possibilities. At some "point" within itself, it senses something—a movement. The movement begins to take on the quality of a desire, a desire to feel itself or to experience itself. This desire is the feeling self making its existence known. The feeling self stimulates another part of the Source—the thinking self—to awaken and make its existence known. In the process of embracing the idea that it has parts, the Source determines that it must be the merged combination of its parts. As the Source is perceiving itself as having parts to embrace and interact with, it calls itself "differentiated," and when it is the complete merged entity, it calls itself "undifferentiated."

The Source decides it would like to experience everything there is to know about itself, so it creates a structure within which it can explore the various subjects that the thinking and feeling selves come up with. This structure is what is called a cosmic day.

From a human linear perception, a cosmic day lasts for billions of years, but for the Source there is no time. Let us say that during the current cosmic day, the Source is exploring the subject of courage. (There have been many cosmic days, and several are explored at the same time, but let us stay within this one.)

To explore courage, there will have to be movement within the structure, and the movement will have to be in all directions in order to give the Source a holographic perspective of courage.

The Source starts to figure out how to proceed with the exploration. It decides to radiate out parts of itself that will do the exploring. The Source knows that these parts will be gathering input within the structure of a cosmic day which is of its own creation, so, of course, that means that they and the Source are one and the same.

In order to satisfy the thinking and feeling selves within the Source with enough experiences, the Source comes up with the concept of radiating these parts of itself through what humans perceive as time and space. The element of time in this scenario is called the outbreath; it describes the appearance of movement away from the Source.

Now the Source realizes that once it has learned all there is to know about the subject at hand, it will need the appearance of return back to itself; that is called the inbreath, or reunification.

The space within which the outbreath and inbreath take place is called the dimensional structure. The Source also realizes that, in order to explore in whatever manner they choose, these parts of itself must have free will.

So, as these fragments of the Source, we have moved through "time" and "space" to experience the full spectrum of courage in every imaginable way. From a linear perspective, it could be said that we are at the lowest point in the dimensional structure we can be at and still be self-aware, so the assignment is complete and it is now time to start our return. The Source has stretched out its arms to embrace us and carry us back for reunification.

Why must our memory of oneness with the Source be veiled? If we knew we were fragments within the body of the Source and were one with everything, we wouldn't be able to conduct the necessary exploration because we wouldn't feel separate. By forgetting, yet being self-aware, we naturally ask, "Who am I? What am I? What am I doing here?" This keeps the illusion of separation real, thus allowing us to explore courage and transmit to the Source the thoughts, feelings, and experiences of all our lifetimes on all levels.

It is now time for us to move with the flow, into the arms of the Source, for the inbreath has begun. We can now become aware of who we are, what we are, and what we are doing here. Just as we must experience vaster aspects of ourselves in order to evolve, so must the Source: As above, so below.

The Dimensions

The dimensions are fascinating. I believe there to be twelve dimensions of existence in this cosmic day. In my model, the twelfth dimension is where the differentiated Source resides; there is no dimension where the undifferentiated Source resides because it contains all dimensions. Within each dimension there are, in my model, twelve levels.

Let us consider this metaphor: if a pond represents the framework of the dimensions, then the hole and the water in it are the first and second dimensions. Now a self-aware being throws in a pebble. The place where the pebble lands is the third dimension. The ripples moving out from it represent the rest of the dimensions. Within each ring-shaped ripple are twelve levels; then the next dimension begins. So the farther through the ripple, or dimension we move, the closer we get to the energies of the next dimension. Eventually, we reach the edge of the pond, which is the eleventh dimension. The twelfth dimension, where differentiated Source resides, encompasses the hole, the water, and everything else.

As we move to the edge of the pond, the rippling effect gets weaker. That is a very important point. The effect of the pebble is strongest at the point of impact, and the farther away from that point we move, the more difficult it is to see the effect.

This should sound familiar, because in the section about reality, we saw how the mind interprets reality and sends out electromagnetic thought-forms through the physical form (pebble being thrown into the pond), and how our experiences (the ripples) are the reflections of that perceived reality.

Many groups of extraterrestrials are currently studying Earth and its inhabitants. One such group, Arcturans, are particularly interested in how we interact with reality from different dimensional perspectives. They have identified three key components; identity, life context, and how we measure reality. Through the Extraterrestrial Earth Mission, they have transmitted some important advice. Unfortunately Extraterrestrial Earth Mission has disbanded, but I was able to contact Kem

Dara Vitra formerly with EEM and transmitted the following information:

> This information was brought through the Arcturans. Arcturus functions as a Stargate into this universe. Energies and information enter through the portal there. This information comes from frequencies of Universal Divine Intelligence. Anything more specific than that is irrelevant.
>
> Everyone on this planet has what can be called a picture of reality that allows them to function to varying degrees in form. A picture of reality has 3 fundamental elements. They are:
> 1. an identity—who I am and what I do;
> 2. a life context—the overall structure I function in and its prime directives;
> 3. standard of measurement—how I determine what is real and what is not.
>
> If you want to make a radical change in your life, three shifts must take place. There must be a shift in your identity, a shift in your life context and a shift in the way you measure reality. These three shifts provide focal points for the Arcturans' description of the third, fourth, and fifth dimensions.
>
> In the third dimension:
> - the identity is, "I am a struggling human."
> - the life context is, "I am here to learn or earn my way out of this."
> - the way you measure reality is, "It is real because I experience it."
>
> In the fourth dimension:
> - the identity is, "I am a surviving or recovering [whatever]."
> - the life context is, "I am here to heal, fix or save myself and everybody else on the planet."
> - the way you measure reality is, "I can feel or sense the subtle energies."

In the fifth dimension:

- the identity is, "I am a multidimensional master."
- the life context is, "I am here to co-create Heaven on Earth with other multidimensional masters."
- the way you measure reality is, "It is real because I choose to participate with it as real."

In most people, ninety percent of their pictures of reality are unconscious. Radical shifts may be made by becoming as conscious as possible of what these three elements are for you and consistently and unfailingly taking action-through word, thought, and physical expression to demonstrate new elements. This requires everything of you. It requires becoming aware of what you imply as reality in every moment. There are count-less methods of affecting pictures of reality—with sound, touch, color, meditation, etc. The impact and effectiveness of these methods all depend upon the perspective with which they are applied and the consistency of living that perspective in each and every moment.

The mass consciousness on this planet operates in different stages of third dimensional pictures of reality, the most com-mon having the shared fundamentals of: "I am a struggling human, here on this planet with my one shot. I am at the mercy of events outside of my ability to control, a victim of circum-stances unless I can manage to learn the game and play it well enough to stay on top and manipulate others to get what I want. If I don't learn well enough, I will be punished. If I do learn the rules, I will be rewarded. It's all about survival and there is good and bad, right and wrong, black and white. My reality is determined and measured by my beliefs and my five senses. If I don't believe it, it isn't real. If I can't see it or touch it, it isn't real. I reference the past to determine my future. It's all about me."

As consciousness begins to evolve, people move through the stages of fourth dimensional pictures of reality: "I am not as much of a victim as I thought. I can control my reality. I am here to fix all the problems of the world, to heal it, and save everyone. I am the Light and I am here to fight the darkness and overcome evil. Or maybe, I am a good person and they are bad people, but I can help them! I still manipulate people, but it's for their own good! I have good intentions. I pay attention to my intuition and my emotions. My feelings and my beliefs determine what is real and what isn't. I never judge anyone. It's all karmic. I'm sure I'm earning enough points to finally get out of here. I'm one of the good guys. All I have to do is just be and go with the flow. If something goes wrong, what does that mean about me? I'll process everything that comes up as a result and if I process enough, I will finally be cleared and pure and healed of all my stuff. Then I will be worthy of Spirit, and I can build my Lightbody and get out of here. I am here to serve."

And as consciousness continues to evolve, there is a shift from the enemy patterning that underpins the fourth-dimensional picutre of reality: "I am a divine, multidimensional expression of spirit, as are all. I am here in this grand illusion participating with the awakening of a planet and the evolution of a universe! The idea of controlling my reality is a half-truth. I don't control anything without the cooperation of the entire universe. I don't exist without every other living thing. I am one with all. I am becoming conscious in the densest aspects of my overall multidimensional self to co-create a new reality in cooperation with the divine forces. I determine what is real and what isn't by simple recognition of truth. My knowing is my directing determination. Darkness is an illusion. There are no enemies. A dance and intertwining of divine love and divine intelligence make up the ever-changing divine matrix of dimensional reality. Consciousness is structural. Grace is present in each and every living moment. I am here integrating the overall aspects of my awareness as part of the unfolding evolution of this universe."

Each of these evolving pictures of reality is inclusive of the lower dimension's picture. The previous identities, contexts, and standards of measurement do not disappear. They are all integrated in and given different priorities in terms of determination. The more expansion in consciousness that takes place, the more inclusion occurs.

We are always working within the mass consciousness. And when it appears that we have gone unconscious, it is just part of the ebb and flow, the spiral movement of the inclusion and integration process. When one person makes a shift in consciousness, because we are all interconnected, it cuts a pathway in the mass consciousness for others to do the same. Pictures of reality are contained in the patterns and information in our DNA. Dimensions are simply varying frequencies of energy and Light. One is not better than another. Do what is yours to do and relax. All is well. There are no false steps. Grace, love, creation, and evolution move inexorably forward. No single individual is the determining factor. Blessings.

Looking at the dimensions in this manner creates a quick reference so you can determine where your basic positioning in reality is at a given moment. Let us assume that what I labeled the Arcturans' perception is accurate. That means that if you measure reality by believing it is so because you experience it, you will stay in the "I am a struggling human" identity.

In other words, that belief takes away your responsibility for you creating your own reality. It makes it seem as though things just happen and you are a victim. That attitude pulls you away from the process of being a co-creator. Conscious self-awareness and participating in the co-creator process are essential for experiencing other dimensions. The more you participate in the co-creator process, the closer you move toward experiencing other dimensions.

I am not going to dwell on the third and fourth dimensions because, in my opinion, they are rapidly becoming obsolete. They are no longer needed, and the more you hang on to them, the more pain the hanging on will cause you. For every system that collapses or becomes obsolete, a new system has already been established to replace it.

I do want to focus on the fifth dimension, for that is what humanity is moving toward. It is imperative that you stop seeing yourself as struggling or as a being that needs to be fixed, and start focusing on what is right and good about yourself. You are a multidimensional master. That is what you are, and you must live it. In order to do that, you must teach your physical body how to accept that much power without going into overload.

Humanity is on the threshold of learning about the fifth dimension. As good as all the books already written are, the best are yet to come. I am not saying there are not individuals who are experiencing the fifth dimension and beyond, for there are many levels of consciousness, and the mind can go to many places. But the experience itself and the expression of it in words can be quite different from each other.

I believe Kryon expressed it well when he spoke of expectation: "When the visionary was pulled through the veil, he did not receive the mind of God. Indeed, he came over with the expectation and assumption. This bias alone will corrupt the perception of what is actually the truth of what is being shown the visionary ... for what your visionary sees does not make sense because he does not relate the reality of what he is observing to anything but what he knows."

Kryon was speaking about the unpredictable nature of human predictions, but the statement holds true also when experiencing dimensions or perceiving points of realization (initiations). The expression of them is affected not only by your expectations and assumptions about the experience based on what you already know, but also by the limits of language.

Each dimension deals with time and space a little differently. Time and space have a geometric relationship to each other. The third and fourth dimensions are closed systems and are cubic. The fifth dimension is a tetrahedral structure, which is totally in the now. It is during this move from third and fourth dimensions to the fifth dimension that the mind becomes no longer distanced from the heart; they begin to work in unison. In the fifth dimension, you will find everything that was and is and always will be. In the fifth dimension, time and space are simultaneous.

As you move beyond the fifth dimension, you begin to move beyond structures like identity and life context. Structures are pure energy, pure essence in form. In this state, the energy body needs little to sustain it as compared to a third and fourth dimensional reality. Therefore, little is created for the self, for wants and needs are few. All that is created, then, is created out of the goodness of the heart and for the experience of creation. All energy is created through the mind of the Source, and it is through Light that the differentiated Source manifests. In these higher dimensions, the energy that constitutes spirit is actually part of the higher essence of the mind of the Source.

As the Source is embracing humanity to return us for reunification, it is also assisting us by speeding up the collapse of time and expansion of space in this universe. That is causing movement through the levels of the fourth dimension so planet Earth and her inhabitants can accelerate their evolution.

As of the 7-7-7 gateway (July 7, 1996=7-7-7), planet Earth had raised her consciousness and resided on the fifth level of the fourth dimension. This gateway made the Universal Mind and the Akashic Records available to all whose frequencies are high enough to tap into that information. The reason many are under the illusion of being in the third dimension is simply that there are enough third-dimensional thought-forms still in existence to allow people to tap into that illusion of reality.

The planet and its inhabitants have experienced the maximum separation from the Source of this cosmic day and are now in the process of returning for reunification with Source. You can make the divine expression of your return a memorable one. You can bring forth your threads of the tapestry that is the divine plan. You can design your intention to live Heaven now.

To sum it all up, there is but one primary intention, and that is to follow spirit without hesitation. Every choice I make reflects this primary intention. Every choice I make is what creates my design.

Epilogue

As a means of reaching completion, I have included a guided meditation that I wrote for a seminar to assist in the Ascension of the planet and of humanity.

Get comfortable and remember to breathe deeply to keep the energy flowing. Take a few cleansing breaths. On the in-breath, pull in golden liquid Light and the incandescent white Light of Source and feel it filling your cells. On the out-breath, release any resistance in your body. Allow your heart to feel the sound of the words as you slowly say, "Great Presence of Life, mighty I AM Presence, the Mahatma, my holy Christ-self, the ascended host, and any angels destined to work with me, formulate the tube of invincible protection around my bodies and establish the consuming Violet Flame rising up through my feet to dissolve and consume every particle of accumulation that is less than my divine perfection, that is not in keeping with the will of the Source in my lifestream from the past, in the present and the future, every cause, effect, record and memory, now and forever."

Imagine yourself climbing a mountain. The air is brisk. You can feel it on your face. Take a few steps and feel the ground beneath your feet. As you ascend the mountain toward the high places, look back over your shoulder. See places along your path where you have experienced the trials and tribulations throughout your journey. Look past those areas to the distant valley you started from. Feel your heart fill with the joy of knowing you have come so far, for you are one of the wayshowers. And even though all past, present and future exists in the eternal now, you have chosen to experience your journey in a linear direction. You have done this so that you may leave a trail, a pathway of Light, for others to follow.

Looking ahead, you know it is your duty and responsibility to charge your being with the purest and highest vibrational pattern, the pattern matching the universal language of Light. You are accomplishing this with your warrior discipline, your unwavering love for the Source, and your faith in the divine plan. Nothing can stop you from accomplishing the tasks at hand which will electrify the entire planet—and beyond—with a new reign of truth and oneness so that the pure energy of the Source can be experienced by all.

Through the mind and heart, you will set your intention. Take a few moments and imagine Heaven on Earth—that which is to come through your efforts and through the efforts of others who are also assisting.

Connect now to the web-like grid of Light around and through this planet, a grid system that is so intricate and illuminated it shields any slower vibrations from entering, and any slower vibrations from within are forced to the surface to be exposed and transformed. The Light of a thousand suns can not compare to this new, completely activated and stabilized electromagnetic star grid system, the effects of which ripple beyond this universe. You can reach out and connect with this wondrous grid to immediately feel the gentle, even flow of the universal ocean of golden liquid Light as it fills your cells, releasing within your DNA the illumination of radiant peace, harmony, and divine love. You know you are one with everyone and everything. You experience the Source of your existence; you communicate with All That Is.

Experience this feeling for a few moments. Allow this knowledge to penetrate your cells. Breathe it into your body.

Now, narrow your vision to a finite point and focus your attention on a specific area on the planet. Imagine activating new bands of Light in the existing electromagnetic grid system. Strengthen and stabilize each new element as you build, making sure it is in alignment with and of the same vibration as the grid now in use. Breathe deeply, breathing into your vision that golden liquid Light and the incandescent white Light of Source to ensure success. Experience this for a few moments.

When you feel ready, come down the mountain and back into the room, bringing with you the joy and exhilaration of your experience. Feel the gratitude of the celestial realms and rejoice.

May Spirit bless you and keep you through your reunification with the Source.

Glossary

Absolute—the perfected total, completed.

Adam Kadmon—the blueprint of the perfect physical form.

Akashic Record*—ethereal records that store attitudes, emotions and concepts of the mind as the physical body experiences tastes, smells, sights, sounds, emotions, and thoughts during each Earthly incarnation. They use the law that states "for every action there is a reaction." New experiences are created based on past experiences as noted in these orderly, accurate records. The sum of these records indicates the stage of evolution a person is at, as she/he progresses toward perfection. They hold the images of all events, occurrences, and knowledge a being has accepted and encountered throughout all lives. They are part of the soul-mind construct. They are comparable to a large computer; they take in exactly what is fed to them by the mind.

Angel*—an instrument of the Divine, manifests no personality separate from the message it bears; serves selflessly.

Arcane—pertaining to ancient wisdom concerned with knowledge of the esoteric world and the inner life, and intended for or understood by only a chosen few; pertaining to information kept secret or not publicly disclosed.

Ascended Masters—a spiritual hierarchy of beings who have triumphed over matter on the physical plane, having achieved this goal by the same steps of mastery that are available to all of humanity in embodiment today. They offer love, guidance and support for our evolution.

Ascended realms— higher states of vibration beyond duality and beyond the third dimension.

Ascension*—the process of purifying the body from gross vibrations by means of righteous thoughts, actions, and high qualitative living; when all the worthless actions, memories and thoughts are resolved and dissipated, the soul-mind in the body returns to its source.

Aura*—a usually invisible electromagnetic, intelligent energy field completely surrounding an entity, living or nonliving, and functioning as a blueprint and battery for that entity. It is instrumental in the entity's growth maturation, cell maintenance, and death. Different frequencies emanate from each entity or system and blend with the magnetism in their proximity to create the entity's electromagnetic field. The entity radiates its aura according to its rate of vibration and level of intelligence and awareness, and the field returns the radiations, creating the entity's body form. The auric field cannot exist without the entity and vice versa.

Beings of Light—highly evolved entities that emit divine emanations and that can exist in various electromagnetic spectrums; soul-minds who have evolved to such a superior state of consciousness that they no longer take on human bodies.

*Brotherhood of Light***—advanced spiritual intelligences that have the responsibility of governing with respect to the local spiritual hierarchy or federation.

*Celestial**—pertaining to the sky; as sky or as visible heaven; pertaining to an invisible world of subtle energies and life intelligences that must be perceived clairvoyantly; an invisible heaven of many levels of energy.

Chakra—a center of energy connected with the human body; where the physical works together with external energy fields to provide a portal that connects complex spiritual, mental and biological networks.

*Channeling**—allowing an etheric intelligence to enter one's field and impress thoughts which can be spoken aloud, using one's own voice. A channeler's body is relaxed and [ideally] the mind is uncluttered and free of predetermined concepts and opinions. Awareness is heightened and the channeler senses another presence operating through him or her. Besides verbal channeling, music, art and writing can also be channeled.

Consciousness—a succession of expansions within a human being resulting in a growth of the faculty of awareness which constitutes the predominant characteristic of the observer within. Consciousness is able to progress until, eventually, it becomes divine.

*Dimensions**—a term used by metaphysicians and psychics to categorize various frequencies of different states of matter. Each dimension has unique living forms, special functions and special laws. The dimensions interpenetrate Earth and its surroundings.

Divine—of or like God, the Source, All That Is; given or inspired by that Source; holy, sacred, supremely great.

Divine seed**—a product of the Divine Mind, which is used for the planting or repetition of a pattern of elements belonging to "the image" and "the similitude" of a divine creation; the product of a divine thought form.

Electromagnetic field—a force field that exists throughout space and matter and that contains electromagnetic energy. In the field, electrical current and magnetic fields can interact.

Electromagnetic universe*—which is made up of atoms. Each atom has an electromagnetic field around its nucleus, making the universe and everything in it electromagnetic in nature. Each atom vibrates at its own frequency, manifesting shapes, forms, colors, sounds and matter of varying degrees of density. The electromagnetic field never leaves the atom; each atom is electrically connected to all other atoms by this field.

Esoteric*—pertaining to inner or subjective information, as opposed to objective information; pertaining to information that can be intellectualized but that will not be accepted by an individual until his or her belief system is ready for its incorporation; pertaining to information that cannot necessarily be proven by present scientific means, the value of which is acknowledged nonetheless; pertaining to knowledge of the soul-mind—its purpose and growth.

Etheric*—pertaining to the invisible world; invisible for most but composed of tenuous matter which, when vibrating, can convey the sensation of Light to the eye.

Eye of Horus—one of the manifestations of the Eternal Eye through which a template of vibratory patterns is used by the Source to generate physical creation.

Hologram—the pattern held in each part of a living entity that contains every element of the whole entity. Throughout nature each part is completely intertwined with the entire entity to which it belongs and has characteristics of the whole.

I AM Presence*—the divine spark of Totality in all individuals, human or otherwise; the intelligent potential in the seed of the human species that gives the human being motivation to unfold into a perfect human being; a sacred connection with the ultimate; one's true Self.

Kundalini*—a concentrated current of intelligent, cosmic, invisible energy absolutely vital to life. It is coiled at the base of the spine and fed by the chakras along the spine and by the cosmic energy entering through the feet from the Earth. As wisdom is accumulated through each incarnation, this electromagnetic energy moves slowly up the spine, directed by the soul-mind as it meets the requirements of each chakra, according to the needs and thinking of the individual.

Lay-oo-esh**—the "Pillar of Light," an energy projection used by Brotherhoods to communicate with the faithful through the harmonics of Light.

Lightbody*—a purified structure, extremely sensitive to the higher etheric realms, that is created by a transformation of dense physical substance into Light; a radiantly luminous energy field whirling constantly.

Merkabah—the Light grid built around the physical form of any living thing, including planet Earth, as a necessary prelude to ascension. (Aka "the Merkabah vehicle.)

Monad*—a concentrated mass of energy and intelligence that contains a complete replica of Totality when it was in its original perfect state and that is endowed with the urge to return to this perfect state, which keeps it in perpetual motion; a unit that incorporates the whole, the exquisitely orderly behavior of Light which indicates the underlying pattern of reality; a perpetual living mirror of the universe, closed off from the others but still sensitive to vibrations of the universe; a basic and irreducible metaphysical unit that is spatially and psychically individuated; a lensless, indivisible entity that is a basic unit of the universe; a microcosm of the universe that contains the whole as does a hologram; the divine spark of God in every living thing that possesses all the attributes of God, which motivates it to evolve until it once again is one with God; an energy that contains a soul/intelligence, spirit/energy (movement), a consciousness and a memory mechanism that holds the memory of every frequency in which it has vibrated.

Oneness—the realization of the one great Source from which all energy, intelligence, and ideas spring, and the understanding that the human exists as only a speck within it; the sense of being not a human being but just an intelligence; a feeling of belonging that occurs in a deep meditative state.

*Order of Melchizedek**—the Sons of Light who have chosen to come into the world of form and manifest the sovereignty of the Source in transmuting Earth. They work to implement the truths of God and, occasionally, even show themselves as a visible order, administering to humanity through the merkabah.

Oversoul—a part of the soul-mind that separates out and stores all the activities an entity has experienced during Earthly incarnations that were handled with the correct attitude, for properly handled experiences are considered to be wisdom and do not have to be reexperienced, whereas incorrectly handled activities stay in the lower aspects of the soul-mind to be worked out; that part of the soul-mind that is purified and shows the perfected quality necessary for the monad to slip into perfect consciousness; consciousness functioning from the level of universal love and wisdom.

Prana—the life force, absolute energy, breath, life, the life principle; the psychoelectrical field manifesting in humans; the sum total of primal energy from which all mental and physical energy has evolved; that which manifests in the form of motion, gravitation and magnetism and which sustains physical life, thought force and bodily action; the principle behind life, the primordial energy found everywhere; a vital force behind all vibrations under the control of the brain; a primal cosmic energy outside the electromagnetic spectrum and all other force systems known to official science. (aka Chi, Ki)

Soul travel—the voyage from one plane of the etheric world to another in mind only; study with the masters at each level during subjective experiences; a mind-expansion experience.

Spiritual Hierarchy—the organization of gradations of power descending from the One which is all-loving, all-intelligent, all-powerful. Level is determined by the love of the soul-minds who have separated from the One.

Trinity—the condition of being three or threefold; a holistic concept such as body, mind and spirit.

Universal Mind*—a conglomeration of all the knowledge, principles and forms, both animate and inert; all there ever was and all there ever will be.

---

*   excerpted from The Donning International Encyclopedic Psychic Dictionary, Whitford Press, 1986.

**   excerpted from The Book of Knowledge: The Keys of Enoch, The Academy for Future Science, 1977.

Resources

Part 1

Awakening Your Light Body
Sanaya Roman and Duane Packer
LuminEssence
P.O. Box 1310
Medford, OR 97501
(541) 770-6700

Channeling Insights
channeled by Janet McClure
The Tibetan Foundation, Inc., 1987. (now known as The New Tibetans)
Attn: Diana Firestone
P.O.Box 252
Youngtown, AZ 85363

Circle of Divine Unity Foundation
341 Blue Grouse Lane
Stevensville, MT 59870
(406) 777-6961

Ecstasy Is a New Frequency: Teachings of The Light Institute
Chris Griscom. Santa Fe, NM: Bear & Company, 1987.
The Light Institute
HC 75
Box 50
Galisteo, NM 87540
(505) 466-1975

Flower of Life Workshops
Drunvalo Melchizedek
(520) 623-2243

Heal Your Body
Louise Hay. Santa Monica, CA: Hay House, 1984.

Hind's Feet on High Places
Hannah Hurnard, Darien Cooper, Ed. Shippensburg, PA: Destiny Image Publishers, 1993.

I AM Discourses
Godfre Ray King. St. Germain Press, 1935.

Light Techniques that Trigger Transformation
Vywamus channeled by Janet McClure. Sedona, AZ: Light Technology Publishing, 1989.

Mahatma I & II.
Brain Grattan. Sedona, AZ:
Light Technology Publishing, 1994.

Nothing in This Book is True, But It's Exactly How Things Are.
Bob Frissell. (C)Frog, Ltd., 1456 Fourth St.,
Berkeley, California 94710, ©1994.
Flower of Life Workshop Facilitator and Rebirther
Bob Frissel
300 Hazel Avenue
Mill Valley, CA 94941

Out on a Limb.
Shirley MacLaine. Bantam Books, 1983.
Dancing in the Light.
Shirley MacLaine. Bantam Books, 1985.

P. J. Deen
2929 Plaza Azul
Santa Fe, NM 87505

Spiritual Growth.
Sanaya Roman. Tiburon, CA: H J Kramer, Inc., 1989.

The Quickening.
Stuart Wilde. Taos, NM: White Dove NM Publishers, 1988.
Workshop information
White Dove International
P.O. Box 1000
Taos, NM 87571
(505) 758-0500

Transcendental Meditation
Maharishi University of Management
Fairfield, IA
(515) 472-7000

Transcendental Meditation: Science of Being and Art of Living.
Maharishi Mahesh Yogi. New York: NAL/Dutton, 1988.

Wesak Festival
Dr. Joshua David Stone
5252 Coldwater Canyon Ave. #112
Van Nuys, CA 91401
(818) 769-1181

We, the Arcturians.
Dr. Norma Milanovich, Betty Rice and Cynthia Ploski.
Albuquerque, NM: Athena Publishing, 1990.

Sacred Journey to Atlantis.
Dr. Norma Milanovich and Jean Meltesen.
Albuquerque, NM: Athena Publishing, 1992.
For other information
7410 Montgomery Blvd. NE
Suite 206
Albuquerque, NM 87109
(505) 884-7146

Part 2

Breathing: Expanding Your Power and Energy.
Michael Sky. Bear & Co., Santa Fe, NM: 1990

Jann Weiss
The Living in Truth Institute
P.O. Box 562
Niwot, CO 80544
(800) 894-5693

Nothing in This Book Is True, But It's Exactly How Things Are.
Bob Frissell. (C)Frog, Ltd., 1456 Fourth St.,
Berkeley, California 94710, © 1994.
Flower of Life Workshop Facilitator and Rebirther
Bob Frissell
300 Hazel Avenue
Mill Valley, CA 94941

Part 3

Kem Dara Vitra
Hermosa Beach, CA 90254
(310) 374-8514

Kryon Quarterly
P.O. Box 1506
Addison, TX 75501
(800) 945-1286
Fax (214) 991-0091
email: KryonQtly@aol.com

What is Lightbody?
Archangel Ariel channeled by Tashira Tachi-ren.
c/o Angelic Outreach
9220 SW Barbur Blvd. #119-344
Portland, OR 97219
(503) 321-5111

Divine Creations Foundation

To receive a listing of upcoming events, tapes and literature sponsored by Divine Creations Foundation, a non-profit, tax exempt organization, please send your name, address and phone number to:

Ruth Ford-Crenshaw
President, Divine Creations Foundation
500 N. Guadalupe, Suite G-801
Santa Fe, New Mexico 87501-1498

or call our offices at
1-800-540-0639

About the Publisher and Logo

The name "Oughten" was revealed to the publisher in 1980, after three weeks of meditation and contemplation. The combined effect of the letters carries a vibratory signature, signifying humanity's ascension on a planetary level.

The logo represents a new world rising from its former condition. The planet ascends from the darker to the lighter. Our experience of a dark and mysterious universe becomes transmuted by our planet's rising consciousness — glorious and spiritual. The grace of God transmutes the dross of the past into gold, as we leave all behind and ascend into the millennium.

Publisher's Comment

Our mission and purpose is to produce and disseminate ascension and higher consciousness information and materials for the enhancement of personal and planetary consciousness worldwide.

We currently serve over fifty authors, musicians. and artists. Many of our authors channel such energies as Sananda, Ashtar, Archangel Michael, St. Germaim Archangel Ariel, Serapis, Mother Mary, and Kwan Yin. Some work closely with the Elohim and the angelic realms. They need your support to get their channeled messages to all nations. Oughten House Publications welcomes your interest and petitions your overall support and association in this important endeavor.

We urge you to share the information with your friends, and to join our network of spiritually-oriented people. Our financial proceeds are recycled into producing new ascension books and expanding our distribution worldwide. If you have the means to contribute or invest in this process, then please contact us.

Oughten House Publications

Our imprint includes books in a variety of fields and disciplines which emphasize our relationship to the rising planetary consciousness. Literature which relates to the ascension process, personal growth, and our relationship to extraterrestrials is our primary focus. The list that follows is only a sample of our current offerings. To obtain a complete catalog, contact us at the address shown at the back of this book.

Ascension Books

The Crystal Stair: A Guide to the Ascension, by Eric Klein. This is the book that put "ascension" on the map of human consciousness, worldwide. A collection of channeled teachings received from Lord Sananda (Jesus) and other Masters, describing the personal and planetary ascension process now actively occurring on our planet.
— ISBN 1-880666-06-5, $12.95

The Inner Door: Channeled Discourses from the Ascended Masters on Self-Mastery and Ascension, by Eric Klein. In these two volumes, intended as a sequel to *The Crystal Stair,* the Masters address the challenges of the journey to ascension.
— Volume One: ISBN 1-880666-03-0, $14.50
— Volume Two: ISBN 1-880666-16-2, $14.50

Jewels on the Path: Transformational Teachings of the Ascended Masters, by Eric Klein. In this book, the ideas and themes introduced in Klein's earlier books are clarified and refined. The reader is brought up to date on what exactly the ascension process consists of and how to be a more active participant in it. Current topics, such as the controversial Photon Belt, are also discussed. This is the best one yet!
— ISBN 1-880666-48-0, $14.95

An Ascension Handbook, by Tony Stubbs. A practical presentation which picks up where *The Crystal Stair* leaves off and includes several exercises to help you integrate ascension into your daily life. Topics include energy and matter; divine expression; love, power, and truth; breaking old patterns; aligning with Spirit; and life after ascension. A best-seller!
— ISBN 1-880666-08-1, $12.95

What Is Lightbody? Archangel Ariel, channeled by Tashira Tachi-ren. Articulates the twelve levels of the Lighbody process. Recommended in *An Ascension Handbook,* this book gives many invocations, procedures, and potions to assist us on our journey home. Related tapes available.
— *ISBN 1-880666-25-1, $12.95*

Heart Initiation, by Julianne Everett. Answers many questions about the process of awakening: Does self-mastery have to be difficult? Why is love so important? How do we become truly free? What are the challenges and rewards of conscious ascension? Meant to assist you in surrendering as gracefully as possible to the truth that God is Love. Related tapes available.
— *ISBN 1-880666-36-7, $14.95*

My Ascension Journal, by Nicole Christine. Transform yourself and your life by using the journaling methods given in this book. Includes several real-life examples from the author's own journals. plus many blank pages on which to write your own ascension story. This quality hardbound edition will become a treasured keepsake to be re-read over and over again.
— *ISBN 1-880666-18-9, $24.95*

Tales and Teachings

The Extraterrestrial Vision: The ET Agendas—Past, Present, and Future, by Gina Lake. The non-physical entity, Theodore, tells us what we need to know about our extraterrestrial heritage and how to prepare for direct contact with those civilizations which will soon be appearing in our midst. Highly practical and timely information, given by a wise and loving teacher. Related tapes available.
— *ISBN 1-880666-19-7, $13.95*

ET Contact: Blueprint for a New World, by Gina Lake. Direct from the task force known as the Confederation of Planets, *ET Contact* is a thorough briefing on how you can work with this vast army to serve the unstoppable movement of planetary ascension. In the process, you will become a more powerful conduit for your own spirit. Challenging yet inspirational, *ET Contact* is an essential "how to" manual for every person on this planet.
— *ISBN 1-880666-62-6, $12.95*

Lady From Atlantis, by Robert V. Gerard. Shar Dae, the future empress of Atlantis, is suddenly transported onto a rain-soaked beach in modern-day America. There she meets her twin flame and discovers her mission: to warn the people of planet Earth to mend their ways before Mother Earth takes matters in her own hands. Be prepared for a surprise ending!
— *ISBN 1-880666-21-9, $12.95*

Voice in the Mirror: Will the Final Apocalypse Be Averted? by Lee Shargel. A deadly radiation pulse heads toward Earth, destroying everything in its path. A benign group of extraterrestrials warns humanity, but our technology can do nothing. Will the aliens risk everything to come to Earth to help? And how will they be received, especially when they introduce us to the ultimate spiritual truth of the cosmos? Are we even ready for the truth?
—*ISBN 1-880666-54-5, $23.95 (Hardcover)*

Transformational Tools

Intuition by Design, by Victor R. Beasley, Ph.D. A boxed set of 36 IQ (Intuition Quotient) Cards contain consciousness-changing geometrics on one side and a transformative verse on the other. The companion book tells you the many ways to use the cards in all aspects of your life to bring yourself into alignment with the Higher Mind of Source. An incredible gift to yourself or someone you love.
— *ISBN 1-880666-22-7, $21.95*

Navigating the '90s, by Deborah Soucek. A practical way to find safe passage through these increasingly chaotic times. Focusing on ways of freeing ourselves from our past conditioning, this book is a gentle guide toward reclaiming our true selves.
— *ISBN 1-880666-28-X, $13.95*

Angels of the Rays, by Mary Johanna. Twelve different angels are presented in full color to assist your healing and ascension process. Each angel has her color ray, gemstone, essence, invocation, and special message. Includes twelve re-movable full-color Angel Cards and directions for their use. Related tape available.
— *ISBN 1-880666-34-0, $19.95*

Bridge Into Light: Your Connection to Spiritual Guidance, by Pam and Fred Cameron. Simple, clear teaching, useful for anyone who wishes to connect with their own guidance. Offers many step-by-step exercises on how to meditate and channel, and gives ways to invoke the protection and assistance of the Masters. Companion tape available.
— *ISBN 1-880666-07-3, $11.95*

In addition to the OHP titles listed above, we also offer the writings and tapes of many other inspired and inspiring authors. For a complete list of available titles and products, call or write for our free catalog. You'll be glad you did!

Children's Books and Tapes

Books and tapes in this category include titles such as *Mary's Lullaby,* and "The Fool Stories" book series. Although primarily intended for children and adults who interact with children, they speak to the "child" within us all.

Magical Music

We carry many titles of spiritually-based music, including both vocal and instrumental types, by artists such as Richard Shulman, Omashar, Kate Price, Lee Eisenstein, Iasos, Spencer Brewer & Paul McCandless, Ricky Byars, and Michael Hammer. A wonderful gift to yourself or a loved one! For a listing of available titles, call or write for our free catalog.

ATTENTION BUSINESSES AND SCHOOLS

OUGHTEN HOUSE books are available at quantity discounts with bulk purchases for educational, business, or sales promotional use. For details, please contact the publisher at the address below.

Oughten House Foundation

Oughten House Foundation, Inc. has been created as a publishing, educational, and networking organization. The purpose of the Foundation is to serve all those who seek personal, social, and spiritual empowerment. Our goal is to reach out to 560 million people worldwide. The Foundation has a non-profit (501 (c) status and seeks members and other fund-raising affiliations. Programs for all age groups will be offered.

Participate in the Divine Plan by co-creating an international network system of educational programs for Lightworkers and awakening individuals. The Foundation helps you in this process by providing and sponsoring programs through our Organized Community Groups and centers. By being involved and sharing, you can manifest planetary' change in service to the Source for the Source.

An integral part of our mission involves the development of a global network to support the dissemination of information, especially through organized community groups. Information related to membership and program services is available upon request. Please contact Oughten House Publications, or call (510) 447-2332.

Publish Your Book !

Oughten House offers its Author Investment Program for aspiring authors who want to publish their books. We guide you at each step and use our faculty of editors and typesetters to produce a professional result for less than the cost of self-publishing.

To learn more about the Author Investment Program and our Educational Seminars, please contact Oughten House Publications.

To request a catalog ...

Simply call us or use the Business Reply Card (domestic only). For catalogs to be sent outside of the USA, please send $3.00 for postage and handling. Book orders must be prepaid: check, money order, international coupon, VISA, MasterCard, Discover Card, and American Express accepted.

To place your order, call toll-free: 1 (888) ORDER IT (673-3748). Orders only, please!

For information, or to mail or fax an order, contact:

OUGHTEN HOUSE PUBLICATIONS
P.O. Box 2008
Livermore California 94551-2008 USA
Phone: (510) 447-2332
Fax: (510) 447-2376
Toll-free: (888) ORDER IT
e-mail: oughtenhouse.com
Internet: www.oughtenhouse.com